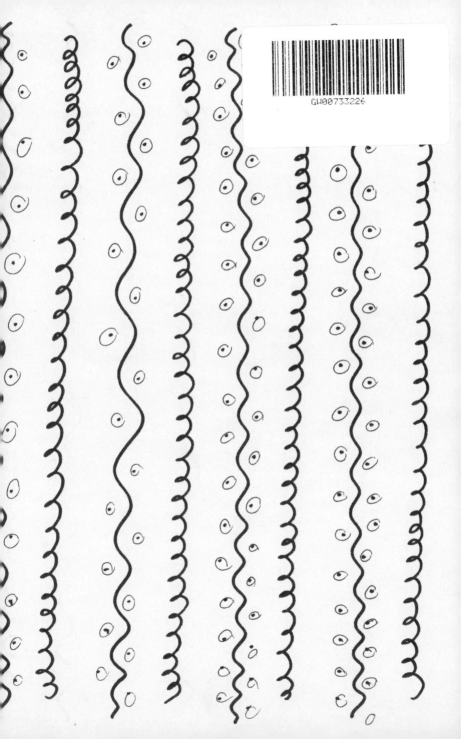

GW00733226

THIS BOOK BELONGS TO

A BOOK OF WONDER

GRAVITY *Amy White*

A
BOOK
OF
WONDER

A cyclopaedic and illustrated volume of arcane and commonplace wonders, as compiled by the editors from contributions received from the UK and abroad and spanning the categories of art, nature, science & other miscellaneous divisions of modern life, with observations by the contributors, who are both known and unknown to the reader

Introduction by Nicholas Blincoe
Afterword by Alannah Weston
Edited by Robert Violette and Jane Withers

Selfridges & Co.
LONDON · MANCHESTER · BIRMINGHAM

First published in 2007 by Selfridges & Co.
on the occasion of the opening of Selfridges' Wonder Room
at its flagship store on Oxford Street, London
www.selfridges.com

Originated and produced by Violette Editions
www.violetteeditions.com

Selfridges Creative Director Alannah Weston
Editors Robert Violette and Jane Withers
Design and Art Direction Kerr|Noble
Illustrations James and James
Researchers Lucinda Parrish and Karen Garratt
Picture Research Jo Walton
Proofreaders Vanessa Mitchell and Samuel Bibby
Production Robert Violette
Printed and bound in Italy by Graphicom

Copyright © 2007 Selfridges & Co.
Introduction © 2007 Nicholas Blincoe
Art direction and design © 2007 Kerr|Noble

ISBN 978-0-9557070-0-1

A CIP record for this book is available from the British Library

The fonts Bubble Bellissimo (front cover) and Black Crystal Letter
(alphabet headings) were designed by Kerr|Noble for *A Book of Wonder*.

Frontispiece Amy White, a student from Bournemouth,
submitted 'Gravity' as her personal wonder, see p. 60.

CONTENTS

LIST OF FIGURES
(contributor name in italic, page illustrated)

PREFACE

On 1 March 2007, a notice was placed on the website
www.selfridges.com asking members of the public to answer
the following question: What are the wonders of *your* world?
For 60 days, this question remained on the website and was
additionally circulated in letters and emails and by word of
mouth. During that time, we received hundreds of replies,
many of which are collected and illustrated in this volume,
A Book of Wonder.

Our aim was to go beyond the usual lists of ancient and
modern wonders promoted by governments and the tourist
industry and discover what 'wonder' actually means to people
today. What things or phenomena enthral, inspire and move
us? What are the every-day wonders of private, individual
worlds, the little wonders that take us - or perhaps just one
person - uniquely by surprise?

Lawrence Weschler, author of *Mr Wilson's Cabinet of
Wonder: Pronged Ants, Horned Humans and Other Marvels
of Jurassic Technology* (1995), describes that surprise as a
'pillow of air': 'those moments of hushed astonishment or
absorption when a pillow of air seems to lodge itself in your
mouth and you suddenly notice that you haven't taken a breath
in a good half minute.' If one is to judge by the answers
received from contributors to *A Book of Wonder*, those pillows
of air occur in response to just about anything from the
alchemical mysteries of preparing mayonnaise (p. 95) to the
efforts of South Africa's Truth and Reconciliation Council
(p. 148), to name just two of the wonders celebrated here.

We thank all of our contributors for the time, effort,
sincerity and good humour they have displayed in their
magnificent replies. We also hope that this compilation
in some small way honours the many and varied wonders
contained within it.

Robert Violette and Jane Withers, London, August 2007

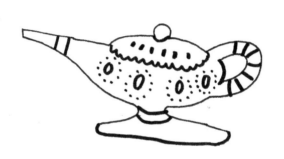

A BOOK OF WONDER
Nicholas Blincoe

Back in my childhood, our family encyclopaedia was a
24-volume edition of the *Britannica*, bought second-hand
from the classified ads at the back of the *Manchester Evening
News*. I remember my father saying that he had bought it to
help me with my homework. This took some time to digest:
I had only just started junior school and no one had yet
mentioned anything about homework to me. Nevertheless,
I began skimming the volumes, looking at the maps and
pictures and – inevitably, fatally – I became one of those kids
who enjoy facts: random facts, surprising facts, *wondrous*
facts. A couple of years later, reading a cheap paperback of
the amazing-yet-true variety, I learnt that the first editor of
the *Encyclopaedia Britannica* was a Scotsman named William
Smellie who chose such a long-winded title for his masterwork
because he suspected that *Smellie's Encyclopaedia* might not
be taken seriously. I have never been able to verify this story.
It is true that William Smellie was the editor and chief writer
of the first *Britannica*, but he was not the owner. The story may
be invented. If I continue to repeat it, all I can say is that it has
the tang of wonder.

I fear this is one of the problems with *A Book of Wonder*:
some of the more wonderful things are often made up. Take,
for instance, the 'clione' [p. 32], which Astrid Klein, a Tokyo-
based architect, claims is 'A tiny transparent sea angel that
flutters its little wings, flying in icy waters, its orange-red-
coloured viscera pumping like a miniscule heart. So cute, if
it weren't for the surprisingly devilish little horns on its head.'
Now, clearly, this is a mythical creature, as real as wood elves
or fairies. It is nevertheless delightful. Astrid's vivid description
will live for ever in my imagination.

Oops!

It turns out that the clione is a real creature: a kind of shell-less mollusc whose feet have evolved into wing-like flippers. So let me begin again. Let us agree, at least, that a wonder is something that catches us by surprise and delights us. It may be something that does not fit with our experience, or be something that we do not understand. Hence we wonder *about* things, as well as wonder at them. A compact disc is a wonder to one person, while another may be more wonderstruck by an old vinyl record. If something delights or surprises us, we may be tempted to believe it is true without asking too many questions. We might simply throw up our hands and cry, 'Well, it's a wonder.' A 'celestial ping-pong ball' [p. 30, pl. 18], for instance, formed miraculously from human hair shaken in a straight glass, sounds unimaginable. I suppose a scientist would experiment and test the truth of this phenomenon, yet I am content to remain in wonder (in part because I wear my hair so short that I would have to use someone else's hair.)

The most famous book of wonder is only seven lines long: the list of the Seven Wonders of the World [see Ancient Wonders, p. 8]. This list was said to have been devised by the historian Herodotus, though the earliest extant version comes to us via a poem from the second century BCE written by Antipater of Sidon (who, oddly, only mentions six: he forgets the lighthouse at Alexandria [fig. 2]; perhaps it wasn't so great, after all). The Greek noun translated as 'wonder' is '*theamata*', which has the same root as 'theatre' and has been delightfully translated as 'must-sees'. Whether or not they all deserve to be described as must-sees, we can agree that the list is not exhaustive; not least because it is centred upon the Mediterranean basin, and is arbitrarily numbered at seven (ensuring that every future list of must-sees only ever contains seven wonders).

Any book of wonder will always be somewhat arbitrary, even flighty. For this reason, *A Book of Wonder* will always be less respectable than a real encyclopaedia. Of course, many

things will appear in both; such as Astrid Klein's clione.
Yet they do not appear in the same way. In an encyclopaedia,
a sea angel would be portrayed as some kind of stumpy
aquatic snail. Only in *A Book of Wonder*, for example, would
it reveal its poetic nature: half-devil and half-angel, beautiful
yet visceral. There is a kind of relation between an
encyclopaedia and *A Book of Wonder*, but it is a relation
haunted by distrust. One is staid and solid, running to many
dusty volumes. The other is lighter, less dependable but
altogether more cheerful, like a happy accident, or, better,
a four-lane pile-up of happy accidents. An encyclopaedia
and *A Book of Wonder* are two different things entirely,
though they might contain many of the same subjects and
even look the same. They will, for instance, almost certainly
be arranged alphabetically.

Encyclopaedias belong to the 18th century. The *Britannica*
was not the first; that honour goes to Ephraim Chambers'
Cyclopaedia published in 1728. The title page to Chambers'
book boldly declares that it contains everything that is now
known, *and* everything that was thought to be known in
ancient times, *and* everything that is claimed to be known
through religion, *as well as* everything that is posited as true
by artists or critics. The word 'cyclopaedia' or 'encyclopaedia'
is a combination of the Greek words for 'circle' and 'knowledge'
(from which we also get the words 'pedant' and 'pedagogy').
Encyclopaedias are nothing if not ambitious, they aim to cover
the entire field of human knowledge.

The problem, of course, is this: what kind of structure
might comprehend all knowledge, in its entirety? What is the
most appropriate shape? The Greek word suggests that the best
shape is a circle, though this does not take us very far.

In their search for the most perfect shape, encyclopaedists
have tended to impose a tree-like system on their subject-
matter, arranging human knowledge according to a number
of hierarchical categories. This is true of Chambers and of
Denis Diderot, editor of the great *Encyclopédie* of the French

Enlightenment. Chambers held that there are 47 basic categories into which all knowledge can be divided. Diderot claimed there were just three - Understanding, Reason and the Imagination - but then included so many sub-divisions that the three swiftly exploded into hundreds. The current *Encyclopaedia Britannica* follows in the tradition of Chambers and Diderot, dividing knowledge into ten categories. These are, roughly: physics, geology, biology, medicine, sociology, art, technology, religion, history and philosophy. Not so much a system, one might think, as a rather tough school curriculum. The very fact that there are so many different ways to arrange knowledge suggests that knowledge may have no essential shape, after all. Certainly, no one has ever agreed upon its shape. Yet despite these disagreements, all encyclopaedists have agreed upon one basic organisational system: the alphabet.*

Our reliance on the alphabet has led to unusual distortions of the field of knowledge. For instance, it has made the aardvark famous. As artist John Fiddian points out [p. 3]: 'Due to the spelling of its name, this innocuous mammal has fortuitously become well known; a lesson to us all that notoriety is not the sole domain of the gifted.'

If the alphabet is capable of elevating the innocuous then it is equally capable of skimming over the serious - such as the question of the shape of knowledge. And if knowledge has no

---

*The title page of Chambers' *Cyclopaedia* describes the book as a 'Universal Dictionary of Arts and Sciences'. From the start, encyclopaedias were conceived as a species of dictionary, which were then little more than a hundred years old. The first English dictionary, published in 1604, was known as 'A Table Alphabeticall', an abbreviation of its full title ('A table alphabeticall containing and teaching the true writing, and understanding of hard usuall English wordes ...', etc, the subtitle runs to more than half a page.) An alphabetical system has the great advantage of allowing a reader to find the subjects that interest them (so long as they know their alphabet). Yet it also pushes the more profound question of the shape of knowledge to one side. The alphabet is a handy system, nothing more. There is nothing essential about it. The first letter of the English or Roman alphabet, 'A', is not the same as the glottal stop 'Aleph' that stands at the head of the earlier Hebrew and Aramaic alphabets. Nor is the order of the alphabet fixed in stone: the Greek alphabet begins A, B, G ... and ends in O (*Omega*).

essential shape, then we might wonder what is the point of an encyclopaedia? If it cannot guarantee to give a full and perfect account of the field of human knowledge, then it is little better than a compendium of disparate facts. A book of stuff. At its very best, a book of wonder.

An encyclopaedia may appear to be more solemn, more grown-up or more learned than *A Book of Wonder*. But there will always be an intimate connection between the one and the other. At heart, this is because every encyclopaedia is a failure and a fraud. Like a comic bank manager striving to be taken seriously, an encyclopaedia cannot open its mouth without inviting parody. Gustave Flaubert noted this, when he produced his *Dictionary of Received Ideas*: a dictionary of what polite people should hold to be true, at least in public. Thus, for Flaubert, a Prostitute is: 'A necessary evil. A protection for our daughters and sisters, as long as we have bachelors. Should be harried without mercy. It is impossible to take one's wife out any more with all these women on the boulevards. Are always working-class girls seduced by the wealthy bourgeois.' A definition so determined to cover all bases, without giving much away, that it surely counts as encyclopaedic.

The tragedy is that an encyclopaedia is always in the process of becoming out-dated. Beneath its bluster, it knows that the day is coming when its mistakes are exposed and its biases uncovered. Ultimately, every encyclopaedia will stand revealed as little more than an anthology of alphabeticised but random entries. In fact, it happens all the time. Totalitarian regimes produce encyclopaedias that insist upon the scientific basis of racism, or the dialectical view of history, or the surpassing wisdom of prophets like Mao and Stalin. Even at their most serious and scientific, the best encyclopaedia will suddenly collapse into nonsense. For instance, everything I learnt about dinosaurs in my family's *Encyclopaedia Britannica* is wrong. Dinosaurs, according to today's scientists, are not reptiles, nor are they cold-blooded. They are birds!

All encyclopaedias ultimately fail. Which is why the greatest encyclopaedists nurse a secret and unspoken desire to produce a book of wonder. They dare not admit it, but they know that once knowledge disintegrates, only wonder survives. William Smellie certainly knew it. He was canny enough to include near-pornographic etchings in the first edition of the *Britannica* and brought more than a little wit to his entries. His piece on horse doctoring, for instance, notes that it is a science 'confined to a set of men who are totally ignorant of anatomy, and the general principles of medicine.' But even the grand *Encyclopédie* edited by Diderot includes, in its section on Natural History, a sub-category of irregularities; namely: Celestial Wonders, Unusual Meteors, Wonders of the Sea and Monstrous Vegetables. Who would like to bet that the monstrous vegetable section was among the best-thumbed in the entire *Encyclopédie?*

A kiss, a spider's web, Pi, the bridges over the Thames, shoe laces, the cold side of the pillow. These things deserve to be alphabetised, organised and published here because they *are* wonders. These happy, random elements support the entire edifice of human knowledge, and are what remain timeless in our pursuit of wisdom.

Wonder on.

A NOTE TO THE READER

Entries in A Book of Wonder
are arranged alphabetically by the
name, description or wording provided by the
contributor. Persons selected as wonders are listed
alphabetically, last name first. Where the surname or
profession of a contributor is unknown or was not
supplied, none is given. Some names have been changed
or withheld at the request of the contributor. Footnotes
and other editorial are compiled and written by the
editors, unless otherwise indicated. Plate numbers
in the margins for select entries refer to colour
reproductions that run consecutively through
the seven inserted plate sections in this book.
Figure numbers in the margins refer
to consecutive black-and-white
reproductions, which are not
necessarily in the
alphabetical order
of the text.
Eds.

A

BOOK

OF

WONDER

'Why, sometimes
I've believed
as many as six
impossible things
before
breakfast.'

Alice
Through
the Looking Glass

Aardvark. Due to the spelling of its name, this innocuous mammal has fortuitously become well known; a lesson to us all that notoriety is not the sole domain of the gifted. *John Fiddian, artist, London*

Abba. Who else but Abba knows how a broken heart really feels - or how to pick you up and get you dancing to forget the one who broke your heart in the first place? *Thom Breslin, retail designer, London*

Aeroplanes. How do these massive things fly? Even when I'm sitting in one at 35,000 ft, I still can't believe it. *Aileen Tolan, mother, London*

AMANITA CAESAREA

Aiguille du Midi, Mont Blanc, France.* The first time I rode up in the second cable car to the top of the Aiguille, quite recently, everyone went silent at the magnificence of the place and the violence of the rock and ice falls. Changed my sense of scale. The 1950s engineers and workmen who built the viewing platforms - perched on a precipice - deserve some credit too. *Robert Tremblay, self-employed father, London*

Air. *Jason Miller, artist, London*

Amanita Caesarea (Caesar's Mushroom). {PLATE 20} So-called because to Julius Caesar, apparently, it was top grub. It's rare and beautiful - a glorious rich orange cap with yellow gills and flesh. Sexy and strange the way it

---

*The Aiguille du Midi - meaning Needle of the South - is a granite peak near the top of the Mont Blanc massif in the French Alps. The teleperique, originally conceived by two Swiss engineers in 1905, was fully completed in 1955. The cable car rises up the north face of the Aiguille and traverses Les Pelerins glacier, reaching an altitude of 3,842 m (12,605 ft) - higher than any other cable car in Europe but still about 1,000 m lower than the summit of Mont Blanc itself.

FIG. 1. AQUAMANILIA: ARISTOTLE RIDDEN BY PHYLLIS (C. 1400) *Jane Withers*

emerges from it's little 'egg' under the leaf mould. Its fragility means you rarely find it in markets. And it's part of the most deadly family of mushrooms – the *Amanitas*. There's something thrilling about the most delicious and the most dangerous foods being so closely related. *Jane Wentworth, design consultant, London*

Amaretti di Gallarate. The lightest and most amazing amaretti biscuits you'll ever taste. *Giorgio Locatelli, chef, London*

{PLATE 7}

Amber Room,* Catherine Palace, St Petersburg, Russia. Magical and outlandish. *Annabelle Selldorf, architect, New York*

---

*Conceived in 1701 by the first King of Prussia, the Amber Room was presented to Tsar Peter the Great in 1716 as a diplomatic gift. Consisting of six tonnes of amber covering more than 55 square metres, the elaborate wall decorations survived until looted by the Nazis during the Second World War. The original panels were last seen in 1941 in Königsberg Castle, East Prussia. Their current location is unknown. A modern reconstruction began in 1979 at Catherine Palace and was completed in 2003, to mark the 300th anniversary of the city of St Petersburg.

Amoebas. *Eve, primary school pupil, London*

Animals. All of them. *Mohanna, primary school pupil, London*

Antibiotics. Many people are *anti*-antibiotics right now, but heck, we'd still be dying of strep throat otherwise. Not a good look with a Chloé handbag. *I. Nasiruddin, doctor, London*

Ants. *Paul Rogers, I. T. technician, London*

It was through the feeling of wonder that men now and at first began to philosophize.

–

Aristotle
(382-322 BCE)

Aquamanilia. Zoomorphic and anthropomorphic vessels crop up all over the place, from Roman fish jugs to kitschy 1950s mermaid vases, but there's nothing quite like medieval aquamanilia. The name derives from the Latin for water (*aqua*) and hand (*manus*), and prosaically these are bronze vessels for hand washing but that gives no inkling of the fantasy and

{FIG. 1}

ritual invested in the simple everyday act. Surely we could learn something from the pleasure and value once accorded water.* *Jane Withers, design consultant and writer, London*

Archimedes' shield. The ancient Greek genius Archimedes [287-212 BCE] developed a concave shield so that when the sun shone he could direct it and set fire to boats as they sailed in to attack. Did he realise he was foreseeing the future of warfare? *Anna Skelton, student services administrator, Liverpool*

---

*Made for secular and ecclesiastic uses, aquamanilia take many forms, from stylized lions with flaming tails to heraldic birds or mythic beasts. One example from the Metropolitan Museum (fig. 1, c.1400) depicts Aristotle on all fours ridden by a woman, Phyllis, lover of his protégé Alexander. Annoyed that his pupil should be distracted from his studies, Aristotle tried to separate the lovers. In revenge, Phyllis schemed to seduce the aging philosopher, promising that if he allowed her to ride on his back around the garden she would reward him with her affections. Naturally, Phyllis arranged for Alexander to observe from a window. The humiliated Aristotle cautioned his student: if a great philosopher can be fooled, how dangerous is this woman to a lesser man?

wonder is the desire for knowledge.

Thomas Aquinas
(1225-1274)

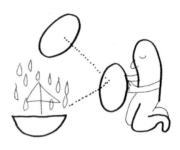

Archipelago, Stockholm. On a cold winter's afternoon, the beauty of this scene warms your heart. *Martin Brudnizki, interior designer, London*

Asparagus. When the first asparagus from Tregassow Farm go on sale at the local farmers market here in Truro, heaven is green and waiting to be steamed! *Dianne Seale, part-time clerical worker, Truro, Cornwall*

Asparagus soldiers and boiled duck eggs. Ingredients: 1 kg medium thickness asparagus, woody

ASPARAGUS SOLDIERS

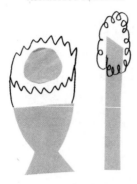

stems removed, 4 duck eggs, Maldon sea salt, celery salt. Serves 4. This is one of my favourite ways to serve English asparagus. Cheap imported asparagus flooding our shelves, way before the season even starts, has made these tender green spears less special than they once were. You can buy asparagus for next to nothing these days. While this is a luxurious bargain, I feel for the English farmers who have put so much effort into growing asparagus for a short five- to six-week season and have to compete with inexpensive and unremarkable imported bunches. This recipe is a simple, fun dish for dinner parties, with not much preparation or cooking skill required - if you can boil an egg that is! If you can't get hold of duck eggs, large free-range chicken eggs will do. Have two pots of water boiling, one salted for the asparagus and one for the eggs. Carefully place the eggs into the pan of unsalted water with the help of a slotted spoon. Set a timer for five minutes for duck eggs, a minute or so less for chicken eggs. Remove the eggs from the water to a plate and at the same time put the asparagus into the boiling salted water. This will take a further five minutes to cook while you remove the tops from the eggs. With a small knife, carefully remove the tops from the eggs, then replace them to keep them hot, and put them into egg cups on pre-warmed plates. Check the asparagus by cutting a little off a thick end to see if they are tender. Drain in a colander, then arrange in bundles next to the eggs. Spoon a little pile of Maldon sea salt and celery salt on to each plate and serve.
Mark Hix, chef, London

ANCIENT*
WONDERS

{PLATE 17}

GREAT PYRAMID OF GIZA
The only surviving ancient wonder, built around 2560 BCE
at Memphis as a tomb for the Egyptian pharoah Khufu.

HANGING GARDENS OF BABYLON
Believed to have been built near Al Hillah in Iraq by
Nebuchadnezzar II (604–562 BCE), as a gift to his concubine.

ZEUS AT OLYMPIA
An enormous statue of Zeus, father of all Greek gods,
carved around 432 BCE by the sculptor Pheidias.

TEMPLE OF ARTEMIS AT EPHESUS
Built around 550 BCE by the Lydian king, Croesus,
and designed by the Greek architect Chersiphron.

MAUSOLEUM AT HALICARNASSUS
Constructed around 350 BCE for King Maussollos, Persian
governor of Caria, by the Greek architects Satyrus and Pythius.

COLOSSUS OF RHODES
A monument to Helios, the sun-god, completed around
282 BCE by the Greeks in a harbour of this Mediterranean
island. Struck by an earthquake in 226 BCE, the Colossus
snapped at the knees and toppled to the ground.
There it lay for more than 800 years before
disappearing from recorded history.

{FIG. 2}

LIGHTHOUSE OF ALEXANDRIA
Built around 290 BCE on the island of Pharos in
Egypt by Ptolemy I, while serving Alexander the Great.
For many centuries, this lighthouse was one of the
tallest structures on Earth.

*The Greek historian Herodotus is credited with composing the first list of the world's seven wonders in the fifth century BCE. However, the earliest recorded list of wonders in classical antiquity occurs in the second century BCE, in a poem written by Antipater of Sidon rediscovered during the Renaissance: 'I have set eyes on the wall of lofty Babylon on which is a road for chariots, and the statue of Zeus by the Alpheus, and the hanging gardens, and the Colossus of the Sun, and the huge labour of the high pyramids, and the vast tomb of Mausolus; but when I saw the house of Artemis that mounted to the clouds, those other marvels lost their brilliancy, and I said, "Lo, apart from Olympus, the Sun never looked on aught so grand."'

Der Leuchtthurm auf Pharos am Eingange des Hafens von Alexandrien.

FIG. 2. LIGHTHOUSE OF ALEXANDRIA *Eds.*

ATOMS

Atoms. From the food we consume to the books we read, our physical make-up is connected to nature and objects in the world on a subatomic level. *Elisa Leshowitz, publisher, New York*

Aubergine. *Abigail Simpson, student, London*

AUTISM

Aurora Borealis. The Northern Lights, *and* solar eclipses. *Heather Ruddy, photographer, London*

Autism. I wouldn't change my autistic daughter for the world, but I would change the world for her. *Sarah Elsdon, mother of three and qualified childcare worker, Lowestoft*

{PLATE 53}

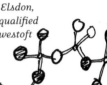

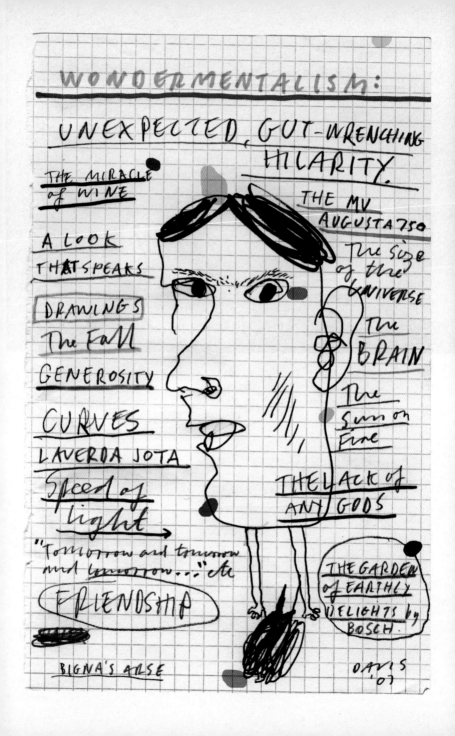

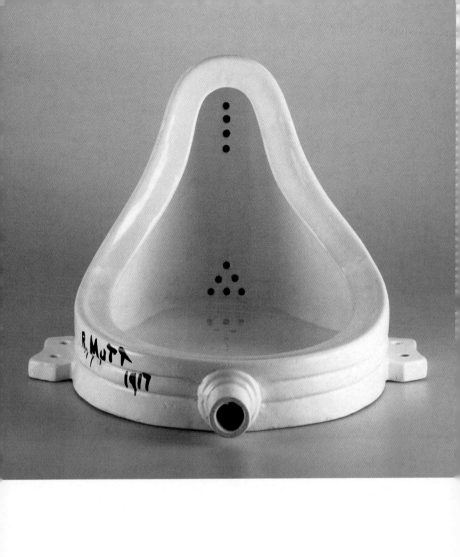

Baalbek, Lebanon.* *Robin Marchant, traveller, Stoke Newington*

Baby (sleeping). The picture of tiny perfection and innocence. *Maria Stanford, human resources director, London*

Baby seals at Donna Nook Lincolnshire. *Sue Stapleton, care-home activities organiser, Mablethorpe*

Bach's Preludes & Fugues. For their deceptive simplicity, they are impossible to play. I can play the first one and I dream of being able to play them all, but they are incredibly complicated. They require absolute precision, and without the use of a foot pedal, they are impossible to fudge, unlike

*Ancient city of the Sun God, founded by the Phoenicians in 5000 BCE.

many other piano pieces. I find their clarity meditative, motivational and beautifully satisfying. *Amelia Noble, art director, London*

aLL knowLedge and wonder (which is the seed of knowLedge) is an impression of pLeasure in itseLf.

–

Francis Bacon (1561-1626)

Bacon sandwich. After an argument, binge drinking or sex, nothing else tastes as good. *John Hart, financial advisor, Nottingham*

Baked Alaska. How does the ice cream stay firm in the middle when the whole pudding is baked in the oven? *Ewan Venters, food and restaurant director, London*

Balenciaga, Cristóbal (1895-1972). Couturier absolute. *Jane Seger, stylist, Nottingham*

Bandicoots. *Dennis Chambers, bartender, London*

Beachcombing. Finding treasures on the beach, making pictures with them in the sand, and then leaving

them for someone else to find.
Susan Gathercole, reporter, Caernarfon

Beads. Brought back to me by my *maman*, my beads (along with poetry and meditation on my Shaanxi opium bed) are personal wonders to keep my sanity. These were hand-rolled by primitive man and found in the riverbed of the Rugnan River in Borneo (Borneo Man were early humans, like Lucy and Beijing Man). *Pia Camilla Copper, Chinese art expert and writer, Paris*

{FIG. 5}

The Beatles. Without their music, our world wouldn't be half as wonderful. *Louise Roe, contact management, Leicester*

Bed. A warm bed. This, and the sound of rain. *Marianne Noble,* designer, London*

**Marianne Noble's other wonders:
'2. That I am half of two people.
3. A glass of wine, a bowl of pasta & a good friend. 4. Music - sharing, playing and discovering it. 5. A kiss that makes your knees buckle! 6. My grandparents (I wonder what they were like). 7. The heartbeat - a wondrous continual thump. 8. Ice-cold beer on a hot day. 9. A good biro. 10. A perfect conversation. 11: A smooth round stone.'

Bedlinen. Perfectly weighted bedlinen - preferably a duvet - so that instead of feeling trapped or suffocated you feel snug and secure but still free to roll, toss, turn, etc., at will, without being caught up in a whirlwind of sheets. And they should be self-laundering as well - every day. I'm still searching, but there was this hotel once ... *Libby Sellers, curator, London*

Bedruthan Steps. A National Trust beach in the middle of busy Cornwall. When it's deserted, it's a true wonder in all senses. *Jo Bryan, homemaker, Peterborough*

Bees (and pollination). *Jennifer Betsworth, creative assistant, London*

Beijing. My photograph {FIG. 4} from 2005, called *Dream of Migrants*, condenses all my experiences of living in Beijing over the years. In this photo you see the past, the present and the future of our city. It looks worn-out, but there is still a future looming. There are details of a traditional Chinese architecture, plus the former

FIG. 3. LUCREZIA BORGIA (1480–1519),
BY BARTOLOMEO VENEZIANO (C. 1470–1531) *Paul Robbins*

FIG. 4. BEIJING *Qingsong Wang*, Dream of Migrants, *2004*

BELLA

Soviet style, the muddy land, people of all sorts, a big pillar telling passers-by where to go, the Olympics, Oxford Street, Park Avenue, Times Square, etc. *Qingsong Wang, artist, Beijing*

Bella. My daughter. She is my most wonderful wonder. *Toby Glanville, photographer, London*

Belly. My belly – also known as the 'line of happiness', which is a sign of maturity and stability. And I think it's sexy too. *Juan Fernandez, economist, London*

Bench, Venice, Italy. I love the posh outdoor benches at Florian's, the café on Piazza San Marco in Venice. I like the fact that a sofa, which is normally an indoor piece of furniture, is part of the outdoor terrace seating. To me that's the ultimate in luxury. More than that, this bench has been designed specifically for an exterior corner of this magnificent building. Its ornate joinery follows the contour of the façade and appears to snuggle up to the wall. *Gitta Gschwendtner, designer, London*

BIRDS OF PARADISE

Benches (plain wooden). Benches that anyone can sit on – what a crazy idea. As public space is lost to commercial interests, benches are a wonder in the 21st-century city. *Andrew Nairne, museum director, Oxford*

Berlin Wall. *Carla Gilardi, designer, London* {PLATE 41}

Big Bang. Really? An expanding universe from something infinitesimally small? I just don't get it. *Jenny Kumar, production assistant, Bradford*

Bigfoot.* *Jess Wells, designer, London*

Binary notation. *Jeanne Tremblay, I. T. consultant, London*

Birds of Paradise. A wonder of iridescence and beauty. They feed whilst flying, flapping tiny wings faster than the eye can see, so they actually appear to hover in mid-air as they go about their voracious eating. *Bruno Barba, London*

---

*Also known as Sasquatch, a mythical ape-like man-beast believed to roam the forests of North America, much like the Yeti of the Himalayan Alps. The last reported sighting took place in 2006 in Saskatchewan, Canada.

BIGFOOT *Jess Wells*

FIG. 5. THE BEATLES
Louise Roe

BIRD BOX

Bird box. The awe and wonder of watching a bird making a nest in a bird box equipped with a pinhole video camera. The way it brings bits and pieces, drops them off and comes back later to rearrange them. *Clive, headteacher, London*

Birdsong. *Danielle Ford,* marketing director, London*

Birth. (1) A living being from nothing. *Sue Douglas, media consultant, Oxford* (2) Childbirth connects with every emotion you have - as well as new ones you discover - on the day your first child is born. True love! *Angela Hamilton, carer, Glasgow*

Blackbirds. Late on a summer evening, when everything is quiet, there is nothing more beautiful than the sound of a couple of blackbirds calling to each other. Are they the keepers of the bird world, and are they telling the rest of their kind to settle for the night? *Carole Robins, services team, Swinton*

---

*Danielle Ford's other wonders: 'Eyesight, our evolved hands and the way music can be transmitted through thin air.'

BLOSSOM

Black holes. *Alan Jones, student, London*

Black pepper. *Hope, primary school pupil, London*

Blind faith. In anything or anyone. *Natasha Lombart, marketing consultant, Hertfordshire*

Blossom. (1) The sight {PLATE 59} of flowers in bloom. The pear tree outside my window. The magnolia, for a brief time each year. And here, in Tokyo, the hydrangeas. *Kathy Phillips, florist, Tokyo* (2) Take a couple of moments to let your world stand still and appreciate the natural events that we take for granted every day: like when a breeze carries blossom across the pavement. *Gary & Clare, recruitment administrators, Enfield* (3) Spring blossom, the few days when it is perfect. English garden roses, blowsy and perfumed. And the chestnut tree outside my window. For 22 years, season after season, it has never failed to capture my attention. *Carolyn Quartermaine, artist and designer, London* (4) When the forget-me-knots come into bloom. *Jenny Kerr, gallerist, London* (5) One of

20

SEVEN
BLUNDERS
OF THE
WORLD

WEALTH WITHOUT WORK

PLEASURE WITHOUT CONSCIENCE

KNOWLEDGE WITHOUT CHARACTER

COMMERCE WITHOUT MORALITY

SCIENCE WITHOUT HUMANITY

WORSHIP WITHOUT SACRIFICE

POLITICS WITHOUT PRINCIPLE

SEVEN BLUNDERS OF THE WORLD
*As written by Mahatma Gandhi (1869-1948), shortly before
his assassination, to his grandson, Arun Gandhi*

the first signs of spring: on
a sunny day, a torrent of pink
blossoms flying through
the sky like snowflakes.
Jason Leonard, manager,
Northampton

Blow, Isabella
(1958-2007). *Philip Treacy,*
milliner, London

Blue-footed booby,
Galapagos Islands. For their
ridiculous appearance and
elaborate mating rituals,
consisting of a lot of blue-
footed stamping, with necks
and bills stretched
ecstatically up to the skies.
They embody some of the
occasionally forgotten things
in life: silliness, romance,
great foreplay and enduring
love. *Karen Garratt,*
artist/writer, London

Boardwalk to Gardiner's
Bay, Long Island. My personal
sanctuary. The boardwalk is a
leitmotif; it focuses your eye.
All sorts of things happen
there - deer and rabbits hop
along, turtles cross your path.
I never get tired of looking at
the different seasons, weather
and seagulls flying overhead.
It's intimate, a little universe
unto itself. The water is close
enough and present, but

there's all this foreground
that is amusing to experience.
It's the path to heaven.
Annabelle Selldorf, architect,
New York

Books. *Lisa Chapman,*
payroll administrator,
Leicester

Borgia, Lucrezia*   {FIG. 3}
(1480-1519). A woman to
die for. *Paul Robbins,*
photographer, Dalston

Boyfriends (old ones).
Recently I have been
wondering (quite urgently)
about what happened to a
guy I have not thought about
since leaving university: he
read Philosophy. In later
years, I heard a rumour that
he had killed his brother -
something to do with his
brother insulting their
mother. Surprising to hear
this, as he was a very gentle
type and I can't imagine him
doing something violent, but
maybe quiet waters run deep.
I wonder why this subject
has suddenly come into my
head. Maybe something has

---

*The infamous and allegedly ruthless
femme-fatale daughter of Cardinal
Rodrigo Borgia, a Spanish nobleman
who became Pope Alexander VI, and
his Roman mistress Vannozza Catanei.

happened to him. Has he died? He used to be very keen on me, but I did not want anything but a Platonic friendship! *Vanessa Mitchell, copyeditor, London*

{PLATE 5}   **Box.** An object of marvellous simplicity. The uniqueness of the material, the folding and assemblage technique are simple. Used every day, it serves its function perfectly, with great finesse. The object becomes even more magical when it is shot with a camera, since it loses completely its scale. One can dream it becomes a country house, for example, fabricated this way, with the same shape and simplicity. *Ronan and Erwan Bouroullec, designers, Paris*

Bra.* *Matthew Conway, accounts payable, Leicester*

Brain (human). (1) I wonder how my brain creates zillions of memories when it itself is made of grey matter. *Nicola Parsonage, marketing manager, London*

---

*Bra-like garments have been worn by women since the ancient Greeks 5000 years ago. The first patents of commercial designs were registered in the 1850s in the United States.

(2) The human brain, and all it is capable of, and how we get through each day and each year, and continue to create and destroy and build and be. *Vanessa Andrews, marketing consultant, Putney*

Brancusi, Constantin (1876-1957). The first modern sculptor? His sculpture *The Kiss* (1908) showed Rodin a thing or two.† *Ben Ruddy, artist, Nottingham*

Bread & butter. *Ashleigh Vinall, art director, London*

Breasts. Mine are sensational. *Sandy Warren, mother and company director, London*

Brian the cat (1996-2006).   {PLATE 16} Beautiful feline friend. Never forgotten. *Susan Deere, civil servant, Bristol*

Bridges. A link between people, river banks, islands (or continents, when they're a tunnel). An essential element in human communication, as much as the internet, aeroplanes

---

†Brancusi wrote of this time: 'Rodin accepted me as a student. But I refused because nothing grows under large trees ... When he learned of my decision, he simply said, 'Basically he's right. He is as stubborn as I am.''

23

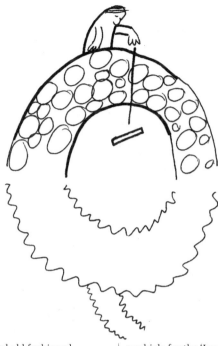

or good old-fashioned handwriting. *François Xavier Anseaume, actor, London / Paris*

British Museum. *Joe Rich, intrepid young man, London*

Brosnan, Pierce (b. 1953). *Nadja Swarovski, company vice president, London*

***Bruce Springshaw's Soul Catcher* (2000).** The sculpture by Conrad Shawcross, a Toyota Capri converted into

---

*Invented in 1957 by Alfred Fielding and Marc Chavannes, Bubble Wrap is in fact a trademark of their Sealed Air Corporation, founded in 1960.

a vehicle for the 'Investigative Bureau for the Location of the Soul (IBLS)'. *Luke Andrews, student, London*

Bubble Wrap.* The most satisfying guilty pleasure is popping a whole sheet of Bubble Wrap when the owner of said sheet is not looking. *Alison Smith, paediatric staff nurse, Southampton*

Building (the act of). Building something from nothing, whether it's a family, a business or a product. *Gill Hodges, hedge fund marketeer, London*

To A Louse

Ha! whaur ye gaun, ye crowlin ferlie?
Your impudence protects you sairly;
I canna say but ye strunt rarely,
Owre gauze and lace;
Tho', faith! I fear ye dine but sparely
On sic a place.

Ye ugly, creepin, blastit wonner,
Detested, shunn'd by saunt an' sinner,
How daur ye set your fit upon her–
Sae fine a lady?
Gae somewhere else and seek your dinner
On some poor body.

Swith! in some beggar's haffet squattle;
There ye may creep, and sprawl, and sprattle,
Wi' ither kindred, jumping cattle,
In shoals and nations;
Whaur horn nor bane ne'er daur unsettle
Your thick plantations.

Robert Burns (1759–1796)

ROBERT BURNS (1759-1796) *George Lyle*

Bad jokes. That this joke still makes me laugh:
What did the 0 say to the 8?...

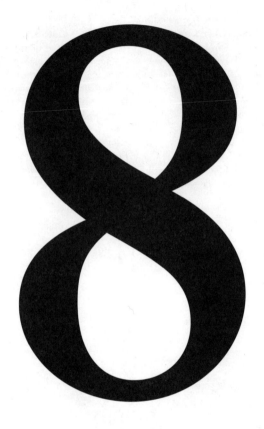

... 'Nice belt!'
David Ellison, architect, London

Bunny. When I am on the train on my way to work I know it's going to be a good day if a see a bunny in the field. *Holly, recruitment consultant, London*

Burns, Robert (1759-1796). *George Lyle, Isle of Arran*

Buses in Caracas, Venezuela. I grew up in Caracas, and its noise and colour have influenced my work. The abstract motifs on the sides of buses, made by anonymous artists, seem to me a distillation of ideas from abstraction in painting, especially modern Latin American painting. *Jaime Gili, artist, Caracas/ Barcelona/London*

Buttons. *Lucy, primary school pupil, London*

28

Cakes. They have little nutritional worth and give no kudos or credibility. They exist only for pleasure. And such pleasure! Let us all eat cake. *Peter Allmark, nursing lecturer, Sheffield*

{PLATE 45}

Ca' d'Oro,* Venice, Italy. The stunning first sight of Venice is a wonder, of course, but, in particular, the Gothic Ca' d'Oro (House of Gold) on the Grand Canal. *Ben Manchipp, artist, Surrey*

Caesarian section. My wife's scar from her C-section. Actually, it has faded quite a lot (I tried to photograph it, but all I got was pubes). The scar itself is a small thing, but, the way I see it, I owe the life of my child and probably the life of my wife to this small line of mended skin. She hates it, but for me it's a reminder of everything that I've got and how lucky I am to have it. *Henry Newton-Dunn, Tokyo*

Canals. It seems astonishing that English canals are still here. They are a brilliant way to time travel, the long-haulage motorways of their day. *Andrew Nairne, museum director, Oxford*

wonder is the basis of worship.
–
Thomas Carlyle
(1795–1881)

---

*Built from 1424 to 1430, its façade was once completely covered in gold.

Canning, George
(1770-1827).* Our ancestor.
*Amelia, Antonia, David,
Lucinda and Marianne Noble*

Caterpillars into moths.
Jeᴀᴀica Hare, ᴀtudent, Bath

Cats' eyes. Not the ones
on the road, but real cats'
eyes: why do they have two
sets of eye lids? *Stacey
Kilpatrick, helpdeᴀk analyᴀt,
Leiceᴀter*

Cats on the hunt.
Everyday bursts of slinky,
sexy, vital energy. *Melanie
McGrath, writer, London*

Celebrity. We've turned
into a race of star-fuckers,
sychophants, malcontents,
voyeurs and wannabees.
But credit where credit's
due: here's to all the
wonderful people who have
actually earned their fame.
*Ben Jackᴀon, chemiᴀt,
San Franciᴀco*

---

*George Canning died after serving 119
days as Britain's prime minister, the
shortest period in office of any prime
minister. Earlier, in 1809 as a member
of the Duke of Portland's government,
Canning was challenged to a duel
by a rival cabinet minister over the
deployment of troops and subsequent
political manoeuvring. Having never
previously fired a pistol, Canning
missed his target, Lord Castlereagh,
but was himself wounded in the thigh.

Celestial ping-pong ball　　{PLATE 18}
**(2007), by Tom Phillips
(b.1937).** A friend took me to
meet the artist Tom Phillips
at his home. Every room -
on easels, walls and ceilings -
displays his extraordinary
work. His latest creation was
a snowy-white sphere he
called a 'celestial ping-pong
ball'. Made of his own hair,
Tom twirled it around like
a drink in a glass until this
wondrous object emerged. He
said, 'My hair, saved from the
barber's floor, is sorted into
black and white. The white,
shaken in a tumbler, magically
forms into a hollow ball'.
*Bettina von Haᴀe, creative
director and writer, London*

CERN underground　　{PLATE 9}
particle accelerator, Geneva.
*Melanie Mueᴀ, art director
and deᴀigner, Hackney*

Chalayan, Hussein　　{FIG. 8}
(b.1970). His table dress.
*Devin Connell, reᴀearcher,
London*

Chambers, Marilyn　　{PLATE 13}
(Marilyn Ann Briggs, b.1952).
American actress and
daughter of a New York
advertising man, Chambers
had already made TV
commercials and posed for

magazine advertising, and played a small role opposite George Segal and Barbra Streisand in *The Owl and the Pussycat* (1970) before becoming a leading porn star. She was working topless in a San Francisco bar when Jim and Art Mitchell, casting their first feature, *Behind the Green Door*, spotted her. They looked through her portfolio, noticed a packet shot for Ivory Snow Soap Powder, in which she cuddled a baby next to the slogan '99 and 44/100% Pure', and said, 'You're just what we're looking for - the girl next door.' The innocence of Marilyn Chambers, however, was never more than skin deep. She pointedly planted packets of Ivory Snow soap powder in films like *Insatiable* to underline the improbability of that early association. She was among the first stars to shave her pubic hair, and certainly the first to have the lips of her vagina pierced for a labial ring. Sometime sex partner Sammy Davis Jr. presented her with a ring of platinum, studded with diamonds. *John Baxter, writer, Paris*

Champagne. The perfectly chilled glass. *Mo Mohsenin, promotions and sponsorship manager, London*

Change lives for £15. In a recent visit to a village in India, I saw the difference that five chickens and a coop can make to a family previously living in abject poverty. They had been given the chickens through the Good Gifts Catalogue. The wonder was that £15 changed an entire family's life. *Hilary Bloom, charity director, London*

Charity. The generosity of very rare individuals - who are happy to give up their time in all conditions to help those less fortunate than themselves - humbles me. *Caroline Lynch, Cambridge*

The world will never starve for want of wonders, but for want of wonder.

–

G. K. Chesterton
(1874-1936)

Children. They amaze me constantly. Especially mine. *Jonathan Towle, marketing director, London*

Chips. All kinds: oven-cooked, crinkle cut, french fries, chunky, patatas fritas. I often consider buying a deep-fat fryer. In my mind, there I am, in my kitchen, preparing sleek columns of various unusual varieties of potato. But in reality I don't own such an appliance. So I then go out to the local chippy, pay £1 for a parcel of vinegar annointed carb and enjoy! *Dawn Blackmore, designer, London*

Chocolate. I love its taste, texture and the natural high it gives me. I adore the aroma of freshly made chocolate. I can tell each day by the smell as I walk in through the door if our chefs are making cinnamon, mint or jasmine chocolates that day. Chocolate is going through a renaissance. I love being part of this exotic world. *Louise Nelson, chocolatier, London*

Choral music. *David West, company director, London*

Cigarettes. I hate them, but whoever thought of putting something in their mouth and setting light to it? *Maria Clarke, science technician, Bexley*

Cinema. The invisible feelings that fill your head and your heart. *Lee Curtis, designer, London*

Clione. A tiny transparent sea angel that flutters its little wings, flying in icy waters, its orange-red-coloured viscera pumping like a minuscule heart. So cute, if it weren't for the surprisingly devilish little horns on its head. *Astrid Klein, architect, Tokyo*

Clinton, William Jefferson Blythe III (b. 1946). With the exception of Nelson Mandela - who should become a saint - no current or former living politician can touch him. Undervalued as the 42nd President of the United States, his global activism continues to change and improve the lives of millions. *Helen Goodman, ex-pat American, London*

Cloudberries. They look like a plump golden raspberries, taste of pineneedles and heather honey, and grow on short stalks in moorland in the northern uplands of Europe, particularly Norway and Sweden, where people come

CLOUDS *Graham Jones*

REBECCA STAHELI
barrister, London

MY
CINEMATIC
WONDERS

That anyone could prefer the simper of Grace Kelly
to the angled drawl of Katharine Hepburn.

That not everyone has seen and loved the first ten
minutes of *Raising Arizona* (Dir: Joel Coen, 1987).

That not everyone spends their holidays
re-casting major motion pictures of the 20th century.

{FIG. 6} Jean-Louis Barrault whispering 'Garance' to Arletty,
in *Les Enfants du Paradis* (Dir: Jacques Prévert, 1945),
while the Nazis took Paris.

Rosalind Russell (1907-1976), Barbara Stanwyck
(1907-1990), Margaret Sullavan (1911-1960).

That not everyone realises that there is
always a perfect movie to watch tonight.

Crying in the dark with a vat of
exploded corn kernels in your lap.

Pauline Kael, Virgil to my Dante.

Muppets from Space (Dir: Tim Hill, 1999)

FIG. 6. LES ENFANTS DU PARADIS *Rebecca Staheli*

to blows over them. Wild-gathered, they have a short season. You can get them frozen, in the form of cloudberry jam, and as a liqueur (Finlandia) – not a patch on the fresh-picked, but a reminder neverthless. I first read about them in Ethel Tweedie's *Through Finland in Carts* – published c.1900 – while researching *European Peasant Cookery*. First experience – love at first taste – came a bit later, while in Norway on the practical leg of the research. A farming family living in the fjords near Mo-i-Rana said the cloudberries were ripe and would I like to come with them to their private patch of moorland. Norway's self-sufficient farmers own their land from the mountain-top (berries, chanterelles, cepes) to the tide-line (lobster, crab, shellfish), and cloudberries are the only fruit you can't pick without the owner's permission. They grow on moorland in the UK, but rarely ripen fully – even if they do, the grouse adore them.
Elisabeth Luard, food writer, London

Clouds. They can be mean and angry and white and fluffy. You look up at them and they come and go. Heaven's in them too!
Graham Jones, London

Coca-Cola. Ice-cold after a hard night's drinking.
Catherine Ricommini, beauty assistant, London

Coffee. *Sarah Stuart, office assistant, London*

Cold side of the pillow. *Sarah Duguid, marketing director, London*

Colour. If it weren't for colour, we would not be able to enjoy something as simple as red lipstick. *Uzma Sultan, artist, London*

Common sense. *Noreen Khan, designer, London*

Compact discs. It is still a wonder to me that music can be 'trapped' in a small silver disc and be converted to a whole orchestra when played on my hi-fi. *Conrad Edwards, retailer, London*

Composing music. Euphoria mixed with satisfaction. A feeling that all is right with the world. *Juliet Kavanagh, royalty accountant and freelance athletics coach, London*

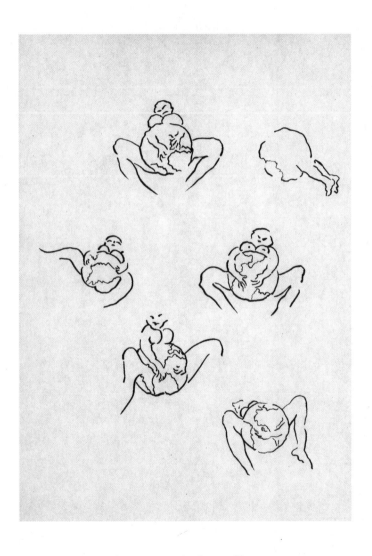

FIG. 7. CREATIVE ACTS *Annette Messager*

FIG. 8. HUSSEIN CHALAYAN'S TABLE DRESS (2000) *Devin Connell*

{PLATE 3}

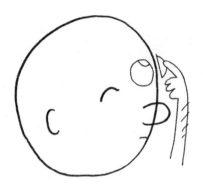

Concorde. A thing of wonder when I was a child, and it still is. How an airplane that was designed in the 1950s could be so far ahead of its time even today is a true wonder. Nothing now or planned for the next two decades will match its speed. It was incredible. Amazing things, like pumping fuel from the front of the fuselage to the back as it went supersonic, to rebalance it as the aerodynamics change at that threshold. *Mark Dytham, architect, Tokyo*

Confusion. There's reverence in ignorance. *Ryan Ras, designer, London*

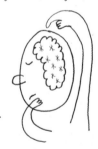

Contact lenses. Being able to see yourself as you really look. *Tracey Yardley, administrative assistant, Manchester*

Contentment. To wake up and just feel happy. *Amee Humphries, student, London*

Counterpoint. The ability in music for notes to play off and against each other. *Jon Gisby, new media executive, Harpenden*

Craftsmanship. People with 'proper' skills are amazing and I wonder if technology will ever really replace that human touch. *Joe Keating, designer, Tokyo*

Creation (of the universe). Every day I am astounded by acts of humanity and inhumanity, and how there is such a diverse juxtaposition that exists between the two. *Heather McClelland, retired headteacher, Northern Ireland*

{FIG. 7}

Creative acts. We all bring something into our different worlds - our artistic, economic, social, chimeric worlds. In French, we say *mettre aux mondes*, to 'bring into the worlds'. *Annette Messager, artist, Malakoff*

Cuvée Elizabeth champagne. Drinking a 1988 Cuvée Elizabeth from Billecart-Salmon on a hill overlooking Champagne at sunset with two good friends. Wine is able to capture a moment in time in one taste and in its flavours are

memories. *Dawn Davies, sommelier, London*

Cycling naked around Arthur's Seat in Edinburgh. Or anywhere, to be honest. To cycle is to be happy. To be naked is to be happy. To be in countryside is to be happy. The combination is wondrous. The World Naked Bike Ride is a protest movement that is growing around the world, but I cycle naked just because it gives me the best feeling I've ever had. *Mark Cousins, filmmaker and writer, Edinburgh*

{PLATE 1}

Dancing. Even though I'm not very good at it, playing an amazing song loudly and jumping around crazily to it makes me feel alive and energised. *Jane Edden, Epsom*

Davis, Bette (1908–1989). From my home town, Davis for me ranks top amongst the native sons and daughters of Lowell, Massachusetts, who include Jack Kerouac and James McNeil Whistler. Absolutely the First Lady of American Cinema. *Bob Sampas, writer, London*

Dead Sea, Israel/Jordan. *Kevin Hall, student, London*

Death. *Charles Taylor, solicitor, Whitechapel*

{FIG. 9}

Death's Head, Woodland Funeral Chapel, Stockholm. The death's skull, or 'Jolly Roger', at the Woodland

DEEP-SEA ANGLER FISH

Chapel. Designed by E. G. Asplund, completed in 1920. The black roof is adorned by Carl Milles' sculpture *The Angel of Death*, with iron gates by Asplund and an altar painting by Gunnar Torhamn. The keyhole in the front door is designed as a skull. You place the key into one of its eyesockets. *Andreas Murray, property developer, Stockholm*

Deep-sea angler fish. Eats things twice its size by dislocating its jaw. If that isn't wondrous enough, it also has a light so that it can see and appreciate what it gobbles up. The light doubles as a sensual device to lure its unsuspecting prey. Flexibility and diversity at its best. *Ab Rogers,* designer, London*

---

*Ab Rogers' other wonders include his daughters Lula and Ella.

Déjà vu. *Naomi Bartle, advertising co-ordinator, London*

Denim. Where would we be without our trusted, loved, threadbare, skinny and irreplaceable jeans? *Sian Meades, classified sales executive, London*

Depression. And no matter how much you study the brain, it remains a puzzle and a mystery. *Patrice Taylor, retailer, Miami*

{PLATE 38}

The Derby (Epsom). I have two great wonders in my world. The first is my family, Catherine and my five children, whom I adore. The second is Authorised going five lengths clear in the Derby this year. What

a feeling!* *Frankie Dettori, jockey, Cambridgeshire*

Diamond cutter. Transforming a dull, rough stone into an exquisite sparkling gem. *Michael Keep, communications manager, London*

Digital revolution. Our work isn't possible without it. *Nick Thornton-Jones and Warren du Preez, London*

{PLATE 3}

Djenne Grand Mosque, Mali, Africa. The largest mud brick building in the world, the Grand Mosque was designated a World Heritage site by UNESCO in 1998 and has been referred to as one of Africa's most important buildings. Built in 1907, for me it embodies the elegant craftsmanship of that time and the town's sense of warmth and community still apparent when you visit today. Every resident plays a role in maintaining the building via an annual festival where food and music accompany work to repair damage from erosion and bad weather suffered throughout the year. *David Adjaye, architect, London*

*The jockey's first win of this classic turf race in 15 attempts.

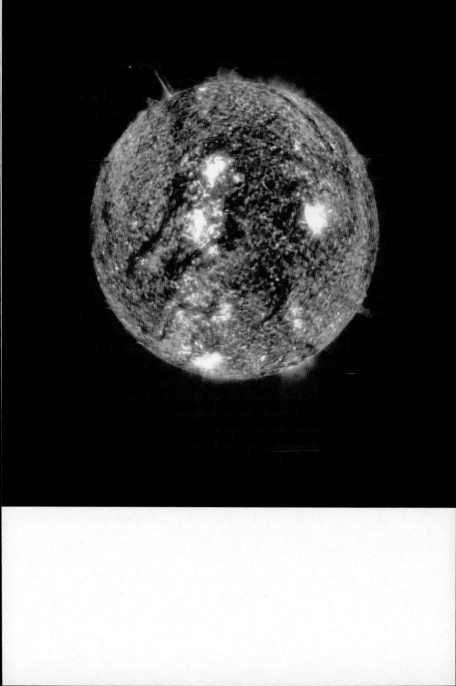

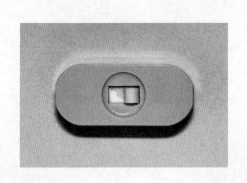

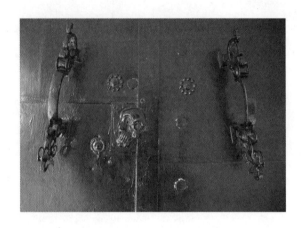

FIG. 9. DEATH'S HEAD, WOODLAND FUNERAL CHAPEL (1920),
STOCKHOLM *Andreas Murray*

Dog. The look of sheer joy my youngest dog gives me when I come in. It doesn't matter if I have been out for two minutes or two days, it is always the same! *Dave Harrington-Wright, Deeside*

Dolce & Gabbana. The Porsche of clothes. *Amar Malik, ꜱtudent, Bradford*

{PLATE 43}

Donaghadee Harbour, Ireland. Previously only ever seen by me as a child in my late, beloved grandma's watercolour painting. Recently I stood there myself, in her footsteps, and took a photo of the land where my family once lived, where my grandma felt such a strong sense of belonging, and that she had talked about so much whilst I sat on her lap as a little girl. My only sorrow is that she passed away before I was able finally to visit that beautiful place. *Suꜱan Cook, voluntary worker for animal reꜱcue charity, Nottingham*

Donne, John (1572–1631) John Donne, the clever and rather callous young man who wrote 'I am two fools, I know / For loving, and for saying so / In whining poetry', grew into the wise older man who said

'No man is an island entire of itself; every man / is a piece of the continent, a part of the main / ... any man's death diminishes me, / because I am involved in Mankinde; / and therefore never send to know for whom / the bell tolls; It tolls for thee.' I would have loved John Donne just for those youthful poems, but I love him even more because he matured. Donne brings a dignity to growing-up; with him, it becomes a noble aim. I often wonder about that. *Nicholaꜱ Blincoe, writer, London and Bethlehem*

Dragonflies. Makes no noise while flying. One of the very few insects to sport glorious gossamer wings, with a dark and iridescent body. *Bruno Barba, London*

Dreams. (1) I once gave birth to a white sports sock in a dream. A very quick birth. I still remember the damp smell and my pride and happiness. It felt so real even after waking up. The fact that it was a dream doesn't matter to me. Now it has become a living memory amongst all my others. *Emeline Coꜱijnꜱe, deꜱigner, Eindhoven*

DREAMS *Emeline Cosijnse*

(2) I wonder at the gift of dreams. See Yeats's poem, 'Aedh Wishes for the Cloths of Heaven'. *Laura Santin, restaurateur, London*

ﻋﻠﻴ

Had I the heavens' embroidered cloths,
Enwrought with golden and silver light,
The blue and the dim and the dark cloths
Of night and light and the half light,
I would spread the cloths under your feet:
But I, being poor, have only my dreams;
I have spread my dreams under your feet;
Tread softly because you tread on my dreams.

W. B. Yeats (1865-1939)

ﻭﻋ

Dress. Stored in the attic of Birr Castle, County Offaly, in Ireland: boxes of clothes worn and collected by Anne, Countess of Rosse (1902-1992).* With two colleagues, I opened one box

*Sister of Oliver Messel, the famous stage and set designer, and mother of the lauded portrait photographer Anthony Armstrong-Jones (b. 1930), who in 1961 became the 1st Earl of Snowdon after his marriage to Princess Margaret, sister of Queen Elizabeth II.

that contained a folded green wool dress with a (possibly customised) ornate purple beaded and chenille neckline. Lying on top was a handwritten note: 'Had a wonderful time in this dress, am ashamed to say. 1941!' *Amy de la Haye, dress curator and writer, Hove*

Dreyer, Carl Theodore† **(1889-1968).** *Alan Petite, filmmaker, London*

Driving. In an open-top car as fast as you can through the deserts of Arizona and Nevada on a sunny day in Spring, the day after heavy rain, when the cacti and wild flowers have burst into bloom. *Paula Pryke, florist, London*

Dubai. The rate of construction. *Will Evans, estate agent, London*

{PLATE 28

†The illegitimate son of a Swedish farmer and his housekeeper, Dreyer was born in Copenhagen and was adopted by a strict Danish Lutheran family. He produced some of the most enduring classics of international cinema, including *Day of Wrath* (1943) and *The Passion of Joan of Arc* (1928).

original light bulb is that it runs at such a low wattage when you look at it. Rather than seeing light, as with modern bulbs, instead you see the bulb itself and its workings. It serves as a representation of the genius of the light bulb as an 'idea'. *Richard Ascott, designer, London*

Egg. A perfectly boiled egg. You never know how it will be cooked until you crack it open, and then you never know how to repeat it. *Alannah Weston, creative director, London*

> He who can no longer pause to wonder and stand rapt in awe, is as good as dead; his eyes are closed.
>
> –
>
> Albert Einstein
> (1879-1955)

Elderly couple. I have so many wonders: Bardot in *Le Mepris*, Godard in everything, the sandcastles of my childhood, Goya, Nature, Fellini's *8 1/2*, the immensity of human stupidity. But most recently, an elderly couple I saw on an island holiday:

Earth. Two aspects: the soil we tread on every day, and the planet itself, especially as seen, and grasped, for the first time we saw Earth from space, in a photo taken by astronauts in the Apollo space programme. *James Roberts, researcher, London*

Earth tremors. In Japan - waking up in the middle of the night, watching the furniture and the walls moving, trying so hard to be fully awake just in case. And afterwards, the very special sensation, the simple joy of being alive. *Anne Ray, imagemaker, Paris*

Easter Island. *Jessica Sands, student, London*

Edison's light bulb. The light bulb represents the 'idea'. What is wonderful about Thomas Edison's

they held each other's hands
on steps walking towards the
beach, taking great care not
to fall, not to lose one
another, to hold each other
like that right until the end.
I didn't have my camera on
me, but in any case I wouldn't
have been able to record it
with all the tears in my eyes.
They were so beautiful in
their love. *Giles Tapie,*
photographer, Paris

    Electricity. *Kate Burns,*
receptionist, London

{PLATE 57}   **Emam Mosque, Esfahan,**
Iran. I used to think that the
most beautiful building in
the world was Le Corbusier's
La Tourette, or perhaps the
Woolworth Building in New
York, or Notre Dame in Paris,
or the Scrovegni Chapel in
Padua, or the Mies Van der
Rohe pavilion in Barcelona.
Then I went to Esfahan.
There's a nuclear reactor
there, and the outskirts of the
city are Third-World poor and
dirty, but at its centre is one
of the world's great squares,
50 times the size of Piazza
Navona in Rome. On one of
its sides stands the Emam
Mosque (1611-29). Its façade
is a fussy collection of

minarets and fairy lights, but
past it and after a twisting
corridor I found a central
courtyard surrounded by four
iwans, facing each other like
four Notre Dames. Each had
a stalactited half-dome.
The domes, iwans and the
colonnades that complete the
edges of the courtyard are
entirely covered in turquoise,
yellow, white, mauve and pink
ceramic tiles. Hundreds of
thousands of them in delicate
floral and calligraphic
patterns. They shimmer in
the Esfahani sun. It's as if
Monet had painted his late
waterlilies onto the Place des
Vosges in Paris. The shapes of
the buildings are profoundly
simple. The decorations
deeply restrained – no figures,
of course, so no facial
expressions, no attempt
to make you empathise,
no desire to get your heart
racing. I found a shady corner
and watched young men
sleeping, women in chadors
walk through the empty
space, their footsteps echoed
twelvefold. I felt like I was
lying in a field of wildflowers
on a summer afternoon.
I cried. The Emam Mosque's

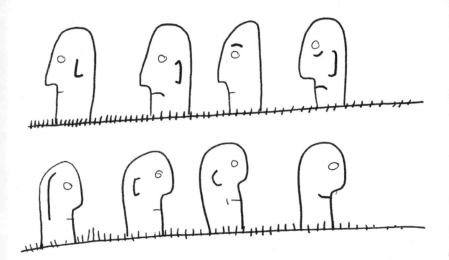

EASTER ISLAND *Jessica Sands*

refusal of rhetoric, its harmony, its decorative abstractions, its nobility and grace make it one of the great built spaces in the world. Duke Ellington loved Esfahan so much that he wrote a song for it (which is on his *Far East Suite* recording of 1967). *Mark Cousins, filmmaker and writer, Edinburgh*

Empathy. When it's needed most. *Donna Perry, single mum, London*

Equator, Uganda. You can even feel a difference in temperature on the north and south sides of the equator as you cross the road. *Rowena Lutu, student, London*

Extraterrestrials. We read in the newspapers about new stars and planets that may support life, and of course about various UFO-spotting controversies. So do extraterrestrials really exist? In the future, will we make new extraterrestrial friends and talk to them over Skype, MySpace or MSN? *Aksha, student, London*

Eyelash. Just one of them. *Alice Bean, student, London*

staring intently at me across the intervening years. He is my great grandfather. What fills me with wonder is that his flint-eyed look of mild reproach is also worn by my daughter, not yet at school but already in collusion with her knowing, watching ancestors. *David Bain, writer, London*

Faith. *Carole King, designer, London*

Faith healing. *Alex Andrews, London*

Family. Parents, brothers, sisters, aunts, uncles, cousins, grandparents and shared memories. *Cheryl Weeks, student, London*

Family resemblance. At home there is a photo of a bristly haired man with a proud and full moustache,

Fatty foods. Why do they taste so good?! And why can't we grow vegetables that taste like chocolate? *Natalie Purkiss, student, Kenilworth*

Feathers. *Catherine Yates, stylist, London*

Fickle finger of fate. *Paul Stevens, optimist, London*

Fidelity. *David Smith, husband, London*

Finding true love. *Julie Hodder, marketing manager, Cornwall*

Fireflies. The Japanese thought they were the souls of warriors who had died at war. *Alistair Scott, London* {PLATE 29}

First-in-line-for-anything. *Jess Wells, designer, London*

Folk. Folk creativity – music, art, architecture and fashion artifacts generally produced by people with little

51

BRONWYN COSGRAVE
fashion writer, London

MY
FASHION
WONDERS

{FIG. 10}

ERDEM MORALIOGLU (B. 1977)
This Montreal-born, Hackney-based 31-year-old
womens wear designer is tomorrow's Yves Saint Laurent.

THEODORA VAN RUNKLE (B. 1929)
The long black dress by Van Runkle - costume designer for the
film *Bonnie and Clyde* - in which Faye Dunaway competed for
Best Actress at the 40th Academy Awards in 1968. Down the
front of this gown's silk-wool bodice, edging its train and
neckline, were calla lilies, toads and frogs handcrafted from
black satin. Co-mingling with the flora and fauna were wispy
offshoots: 'Long black shiny grasses,' explained Van Runkle.
'It was so far out.'

MANOLO BLAHNIK (B. 1942)
No luxury footwear designer can challenge the maestro's
creative expertise. He's a living legend, while his London shop
on Old Church Street is the world's finest shoe boutique.

LILY ET CIE, LOS ANGELES
Rita Watnick's Beverly Hills vintage emporium is a gateway to
her collection of 500,000 prime, one-of-a-kind vintage pieces.
Browse the racks laden with 1970s YSL and 1980s Versace and
there's no looking forward. The past is just too delicious.

ANGELA MISSONI (B. 1958),
whose women's wear collections continue to define
effortless modern chic.

HELMUT NEWTON (1920-2004)
The late photographer's flair for portraying stylish sex
appeal remains unrivalled.

BELMACZ
Sharp, chic, 21st-century, modern, cool semi-precious and
precious jewelry. Produced by London aesthete Julia
Muggenburg, Belmacz fits a princess or a rock star.

FIG. 10. ERDEM MORALIOGLU (B. 1977) *Bronwyn Cosgrave*

or no academic artistic training, and which often describe activities that originate from the beliefs and opinions of ordinary people. They reflect craft traditions of different social groups. *Paul Heber-Percy and Simon Moretti, artist-curators, Paris*

Food chain. Where does our food come from? Africa, India, Europe, Asia? Is there anything we can't get 365 days a year? Strawberries in winter, lamb in autumn, pumpkin in summer, peaches in spring. Hot Cross Buns = Anytime! (Whatever happened to getting excited that Easter was coming?) Supply Chain = Accessibility/Unlimited Choice. Having it all = Greed. Transport = Huge Food Miles. Why is ethically sourced and organic food so inaccessible? Will people ever change their outlook or are we too far gone? *Nikki Tadema, brand manager, London*

Football. *Simeon, primary school pupil, London*

Forbidden City, Beijing. During a rain storm – nobody there, apart from the ghosts of courtesans. *Anne Ray, imagemaker, Paris*

*Fouettés (en tournant).** A ballerina executing 32 perfect *fouettés* as Odile in *Swan Lake*. I've seen Darcey Bussell talk about it, Alina Cojocaru fail abysmally and Tamara Rojo achieve them faultlessly! *Michael Keep, communications manager, London*

Fountain (1917), by Marcel [PLATE 10] Duchamp (1887-1968). The end and the beginning of art. What else could be made at a time of world war? *Michael Edwards, student, London*

Fragments d'un discours amoureux (A Lover's Discourse: Fragments), by Roland Barthes (1915-80). A dazzling 'primer' for every moment you are in love, from the very beginning to the very end. From the first thrill to grief, or exasperation, or emptiness. (And yes, between grief and nothing, I will take grief.) *Anne Deniau, Paris*

---

*In classical ballet, *fouettés* are the repeated whipping motion of one leg, which turns the body on the supporting foot, rising *en pointe* at the completion of one revolution. Accomplished first in 1893 by prima ballerina Pierina Legnani of the Russian Imperial Ballet, in the coda of *Cinderella*.

FICKLE FINGER OF FATE

Paul Stevens

Franklin, Benjamin (1706-1790). Inventor (lightning rod, bifocals, catheter, etc, all intentionally never patented), scholar (founder of the American Philosophical Society), politician (a Founding Father of the US!), printer/publisher, wit and diplomat. He deservedly gets his face on the $100 bill. *Robert Tremblay, self-employed father, London*

Freecycle Network. Belonging to Freecycle enables you to give something back to your community. You find things you need and get rid of things you don't, knowing you have made someone happy and helped the planet. You get back more than you give, if you do it from the heart, and you might just make a big difference without knowing. *Cathy MacLennan, homeless men support worker, Manchester*

Friday evening. Shutting down that computer

and walking out of that office on a Friday is, at once, the greatest feeling of freedom and achievement. *Pernilla Ingram, accountant, London*

Friskar scissors. The tools I work with: my Friskar scissors that I cut paper with and my Felco garden shears that I cut basswood with while making models. Both of these tools are very well designed and fit my hands beautifully. *Craig Webb, architect, Los Angeles*

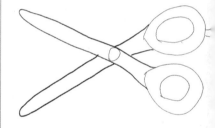

Full moon. Accompanied by the smell of burning wood, on a clear, cold winter night. *Jade Trimbee, radio marketing executive, London*

{PLATE 50}

Gabrielle d'Estrées et une de ses soeurs (c. 1594). This enigmatic painting by an unknown student of Fontainebleau conjures up endless scenarios and possibilities. A real curiosity, intriguing and fascinating, one of the Louvre's less recognisable wonders. *Lucy Willis, press officer, London*

Garden. My garden is small but beautiful and tranquil, with birds flying in and out all day. It relaxes me completely. *Tina Darch, administrator, Cannington*

{FIG. 12}

Gardner, Ava (1922–90). Ava Gardner was, I suggest, the most beautiful woman in modern times. When Mickey Rooney first saw her, 'Everything in me stopped. My heart. My breathing. My thinking.' According to the musician Artie Shaw, 'She was the most beautiful creature you ever saw.' According to the great cameraman, Jack Cardiff (himself something of a marvel) she was 'very beautiful, with a wonderful sexy voice and an extraordinary way of moving, like a cat.' Hundreds of further testimonials can easily be produced. Howard Hughes was obsessed with her. She drove Frank Sinatra to attempt suicide. *Robert Irwin, writer and editor, London*

Gates at the Peggy Guggenheim Collection, Venice, Italy. The metal gates at the entrance to Palazzo Venier dei Leoni, with coloured glass objects, has always fascinated me. When travelling to Venice earlier this year, this was my first stop. *Martin Brudnizki, interior designer, London*

Giant Squid. A giant squid was caught in February. If you made calamari from it the rings would be the size of tractor tyres! *Sophie Groves, recruitment agent, London*

Giggles. A case of the giggles! Laughing at something that's often not really that funny, and being able to laugh at yourself. *Jessica Graham, events co-ordinator, London*

{PLATE 42}

Giselle. The ballet by Mats Ek, performed by Nicolas Le Riche and Marie-Agnès Gillot at the Paris Opéra. *Anne Deniau, Paris*

Glastonbury, Somerset, England. Watching the sun rise over the prehistoric stone circle during the music festival. *Harry Sprout, international hipster, London*

Global warming. *Archie, primary school pupil, London*

Gobi Desert, China. As viewed from a rickety train - nature and technology fused. *Jane Forrester, fashion events organiser, London*

God. *Pippa Gainer, school nurse, London*

Golf courses. A mixture of great weather and tropical vegetation. *Johan Coetser, engineer, Qatar*

Google. The new wonder of the world, but I'm sure everyone already knows that. *Carrie Pilto, curator and editor, San Francisco*

Goree, Senegal. The most beautiful place on earth (at least from teen memory). *Yann Perreau, writer and editor, Paris*

The purpose of art is the lifelong construction of a state of wonder.
—
Glenn Gould
(1932-1982)

Grandad. Who, at 101 this year, makes the best macaroni cheese I have ever tasted! *Jessica Graham, events co-ordinator, London*

Grand Canyon, Colorado River, Arizona. The air, the heat, the vast distance across, the mile down, the donkey ride back up. *Noreen Khan, designer, London*

{PLATE 49

Grandparents. Joyce and Dan Potter, my grandparent, are the wonder of my world, as they have both just recently celebrated 60 years of marriage, their diamond anniversary, and I love them very much. My grandfather was a prisoner of war in Japan and helped to build the bridge over the River Kwai. He is now 92

{FIG. 11}

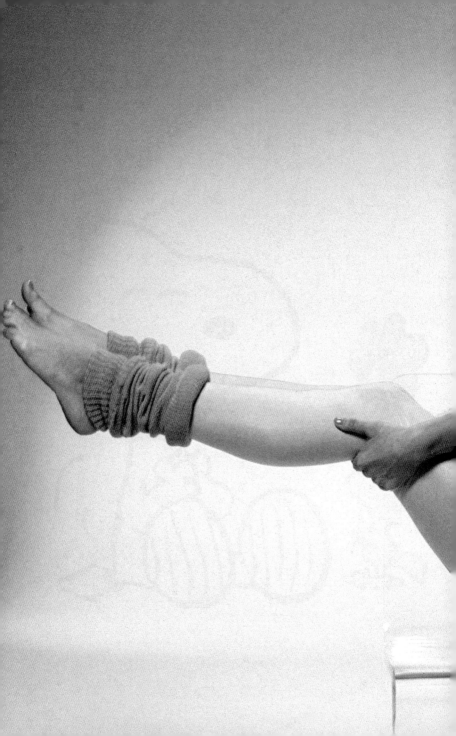

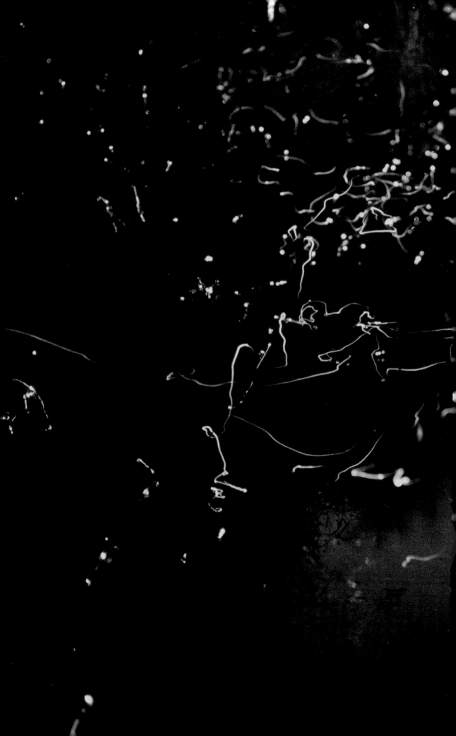

GOD *Pippa Gainer*

years young!* *Lisa Santi, beauty specialist, Trafford*

Grass, freshly cut. Cut grass! It's amazing how this one smell can cheer you up and remind you of so many memories. *Stacey Kilpatrick, helpdesk analyst, Leicester*

Graveyards. Graveyards have a calming effect, which allows you to become reflective. *Where are they now, where will I go?* Not only do you wonder about loved ones, it also makes you think about people from other

periods. *Amber Rowlands, photographer, London*

Gravity. *Amy White, student, Bournemouth*

Great Wall of China. (1) Who cares if it isn't visible from space?† It commands attention and standing on top of the monument is majestic and magical. *Nancy Wainscoat, public relations manager, London.* (2) Did they make the bricks before they started, or as they went along? *Mary Green, recruitment agent, Leicester*

---

*Lisa Santi submitted this wonder on 30 April 2007. On 28 June, Ms Santi emailed the editors to say that her 'grandad passed away at the weekend.' In a subsequent letter - which accompanied the army photo of her grandad, Pt. Daniel Potter, reproduced opposite - Ms Santi wrote: 'My grandfather was in the army for nine years - a Japanese prisoner of war for 3 1/2 years. He went into the army weighing 15 stone 10 lbs and when he came out, he weighed only 8 stone 5 lbs. It was a testament to how strong he was to have survived the whole ordeal, as many of his friends did not. He told me some amazing stories of his times as a POW, and building the bridge over the River Kwai. I hope you use these photos. I know he'd be really honoured. My grandparents never had much money, but I couldn't have had a better childhood, with them every weekend looking after me and my sister. My grandmother, 85, has Alzheimer's, and

lives in a care home. She doesn't know who I am. I still go and see her every week. My grandfather, as you know, passed away only last week aged 92. He was looking after my grandmother himself until only a few weeks ago, when he became worn out, and couldn't copy any more. (He was very proud - he didn't want any help.) I feel very lucky to have had such caring, generous, kind, thoughtful, gentle and truly wonderful grandparents. Yours sincerely, L. Santi'

†Contrary to popular belief and according to NASA, neither the Great Wall of China nor any other man-made object is visible with the naked eye from space. The first photographic evidence that parts of the Great Wall of China might be visible from low Earth orbit was obtained in 2004 with a powerful 180 mm lens by Commander Leroy Chiao aboard the International Space Station.

FIG. 11. GRANDPARENTS *Lisa Santi*
(*Pt. Daniel Potter - middle row, 1st from left - 14 March 1940*)

And did those feet in ancient time
Walk upon England's mountains green?
And was the holy Lamb of God
On England's pleasant pastures seen?

And did the Countenance Divine
Shine forth upon our clouded hills?
And was Jerusalem builded here
Among these dark Satanic Mills?

Bring me my Bow of burning gold;
Bring me my Arrows of desire;
Bring me my Spear; O clouds unfold!
Bring me my Chariot of fire!

I will not cease from Mental Fight
Nor shall my Sword sleep in my hand,
Till we have built Jerusalem
In England's green and pleasant land.

William Blake (1757–1827)*

*Blake's poem 'Jerusalem' was inspired by the legend
that Jesus, accompanied by Joseph of Arimathea,
once visited the English town of **Glastonbury**,
Harry Sprout's wonder (p. 58).

FIG. 12. AVA GARDNER (1922–1990) *Robert Irwin*

GREENFLIES

Greenflies. How can all its vital organs squeeze into such a minute being? Although it is one millionth of the size of a human, when it lands on your hand you can still feel its delicate legs tickling your skin. *Rachael Garland, student, York*

Green traffic lights. *Nancy Gallagher, photographer, London*

Guillem, Sylvie (b. 1965). In mid-flight. Sylvie Guillem is the most enthralling, dexterous dancer in the world. Seeing her perform captivates and entrances me in the most spellbinding way possible! *Gerry Fox, filmmaker, London*

GUYS WITH GUITARS

Guillotine (bagel). No sharp knives in the morning. I just pop in my bagel, slice it easily, stick it in the toaster. Spread it, eat it, easy. *Niki Moore, store manager, Hersham*

Gutenberg Bible {PLATE 61}
(1452-1455). *Pat Gerstner, printer, London*

Guys with guitars. {PLATE 40}
Guys with guitars! Why is it that guys with guitars make me go weak at the knees. It's an unexplainable wonder, but I'm not complaining! *Felicity Hollis, switchboard operator, Leicester*

Hanabi (fireworks). Like *hanabi*, it's name in Japanese, meaning 'flower fire', fireworks combine two natural wonders in one. Exploding with an amazing big bang into a visual feast of colourful glitter balls in the wide open sky only to disappear into nothing within a glance - was it real? And then disbelief as we stare into the sky trying to visualise it again when Bang! the next one puts us in awe... so simple, yet we are endlessly attracted to it. *Astrid Klein, architect, Tokyo*

Handles (of household detergent bottles). Once their forms are isolated and severed from their function, you realise just how simultaneously benign, extraordinary and peculiar their designs are. Placement is ambiguous, they feel equally at home floating, grasping and feeling their way round, above and below sea level. Could they be the strange inhabitants of the lowest depths of the ocean or would you stumble across them in the outermost parts of the earth's crust? *Aishleen Lester, artist, London*

Hands. 'I know something {FIG. 13} like the back of my hands...' Yes, but how well do you really know them? Take a moment's pause, look at your hands, play with them, experiment with movement. Thank your god that you have them and that they do your bidding... and then wonder in awe at the rest of your body. Prepare to be amazed. We take so much for granted. *Julia Frances, therapist, London*

Happiness. It's different for everyone. Impossible to define, pursued for thousands of years. Philosophers, artists, musicians and writers have all used it as a core theme in their work, yet no two find it in the same place. Some find it through travel or through material

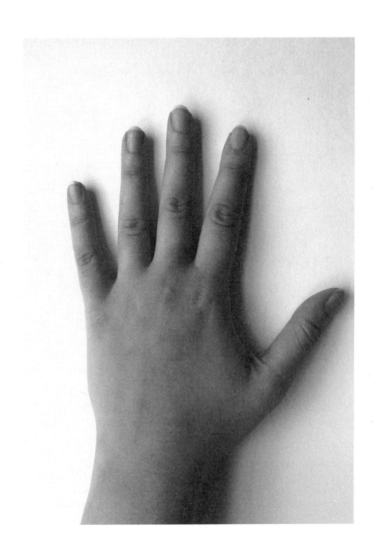

FIG. 13. HANDS *Julia Frances*

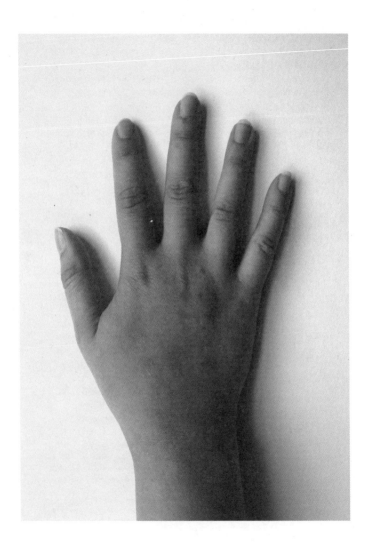

possessions; some through friends, through love, through meditation; and others through food, film, art, sex, drugs or music. However each of us finds it, surely it is the greatest wonder of all. *Simon Manchipp, design director, London*

Harvest moon. On a clear night with a pair of ordinary binoculars. *Richard Sanderson, menswear buyer, London*

Headphones. *Noreen Khan, designer, London*

Heartbreak. *Anonymous, London*

Hearts. My nickname is 'Lisa Loveheart' because I love anything with hearts on. I have a whole house of hearts: bed, wedding ring, clothing, shoes, handbags,

perfume and lots lots more! *Lisa Santi, beauty specialist, Trafford*

High heels. The right pair of heels on a woman can convert you from a Vera to a Vixen. *Lisa Gaines,* marketing assistant, London*

Hinoki bath. A Japanese hinoki wood bath tub (*O furo*) made of cypress, for their extremely pleasant smell when filled up with hot water, their softness and their very simple design. *Laurence Boulet, communications director, Lausanne*

Hirsute people. I'm quite hairy – and I have always marvelled at the *really* hairy folk in history, like Petrus Gonzales, the so-called 'Wild Man from the Canaries'. His entire body and face was covered in long, soft, wavy hair. Or, in the 19th century, the 'Hairy Family of Burma' and the Russian Theodore Petroff, later known as 'Jo-Jo, the dog-faced boy'. *Joel Silver, photographer, London*

{FIG. 14}

---

*Lisa Gaines' other wonders are: 'Make-up (it's amazing how much confidence it can give someone); Jennifer Lopez's body; suck-your-tummy-in pants; diamonds, because they are a girl's best friend; and, lastly, meringue.'

FIG. 14. HIRSUTE PEOPLE (WILD MAN FROM THE CANARIES) *Joel Silver*

FIG. 15. JOHN HOLMES (1948-1988) *John Baxter*

Holidays. There's nothing like the buzz of booking a holiday, packing your suitcase, exchanging some money, searching for your passport, off to the airport and a few hours later – Sunshine! *Chris Barrand, payroll administrator, Leicester*

{FIG. 15}

Holmes, John C. (John Curtis Estes) (aka Johnny Wadd, John Duval, Big John Fallus, John Helms, Big John Holmes, John Curtis Holmes, Bigg John, John Rey) (1944–1988). The pre-eminent male porn performer of the 1970s. In *Around the World with Johnny Wadd* (1975) Holmes brags, 'I'm one of the wonders of the world. I have the biggest cock in the world, and I've been using it since I was seven years old. It's been inside 10,000 women at least, and none of them has been unsatisfied.' Estimates of his dimensions varied. His wife described coming home to find him measuring his penis. 'It goes from five inches to ten,' he told her. 'Ten inches long! Four inches around!' Later the figure was inflated to 12 inches, then 13. His life

and death inspired the films *Boogie Nights* (1997) and *Wonderland* (2003). *John Baxter, writer, Paris*

Hope. Without hope nothing begins or ends. Ideas, dreams and needs, all go unrequited. There is no remedy for its absence but hope. And when taking the next breath or leaving it are the same, hope is the tie-breaker. Hope is everything. *Christopher Violette, music supervisor, Los Angeles*

Hope Diamond.*   {PLATE 25}
Mary Sellers, fashion assistant, London

Horse-drawn hearse. So slender, a Victorian lattice of glass and black-painted

---

*Mined in India in the 1660s, or (according to legend) stolen from the eye of a Hindu idol, the Hope Diamond weighs 45.52 carats. It is believed to have passed through the hands of Marie-Antoinette, revolutionary thieves, and George IV. Henry Hope acquired it in 1812, and it has been owned subsequently by Pierre Cartier and by America's most famous diamond specialist, the late Harry Winston, who in 1958 donated the Hope Diamond to the Smithsonian Institution, sending it to the collection in a brown paper bag by ordinary mail. Valued at more than US $250m, it is ten times smaller than the British Crown's 530-carat Star of Africa.

♥LISA♥
♥LOVEHEART♥

HEARTS *Lisa Santi*

steel. Such a delicate boat in which to cross the Styx. *Simon Withers, designer, London*

Hot-air balloons. From the giant ones in summer racing over the South Downs to the little ones – Kongming lanterns – released in Banda Aceh to memorialise victims of the 2004 tsunami. *George Minetti, musician, Salisbury*

Hot-buttered toast and jam. How is it that something so simple tastes so good and makes you feel snuggly inside? *Karen Walkden, housewife, Braintree*

Housewives. My wife in particular, sure, but all of them. I'm talking about full-time, old-fashioned housewives who spend their lives creating a world for their husbands and children. The feminists make them out to be fools. The movies make them out to be bullies and scolds. They're supposed to be out-of-date, unempowered, politically incorrect and not much fun. But the ones I know are amazingly happy. And their husbands think they hung the moon. *Andrew Klavan, writer, Santa Barbara*

Hugging. *Michael Violette, primary school pupil, London*

Human flight. A vision of a future of humanity, where everybody can be happy, living together in peace, and thus 'learn how to fly' – metaphorically. *Reinhard Schleining, illustrator, London*

Human genome. *Ryan Ras, designer, London*

{FIG. 16}

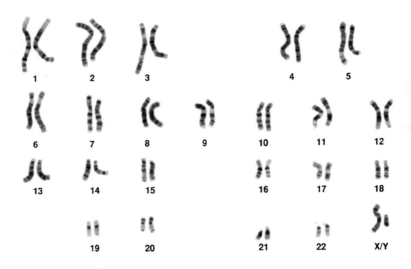

FIG. 16. HUMAN GENOME *Ryan Ras*

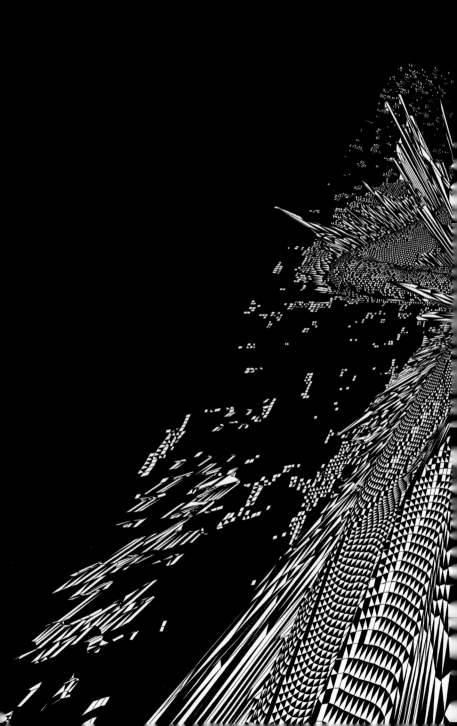

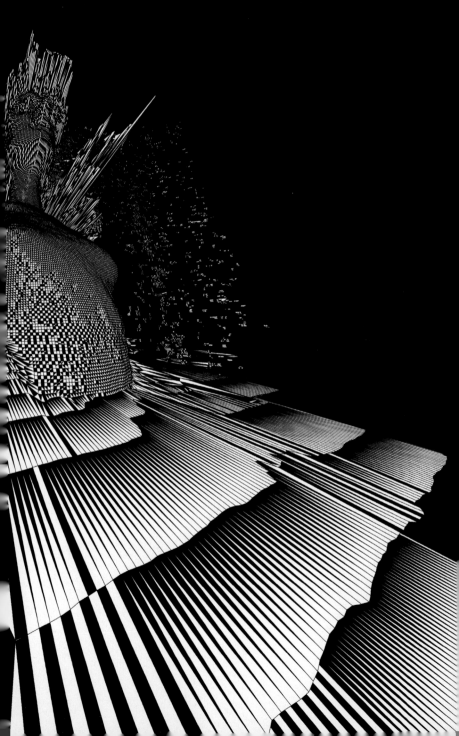

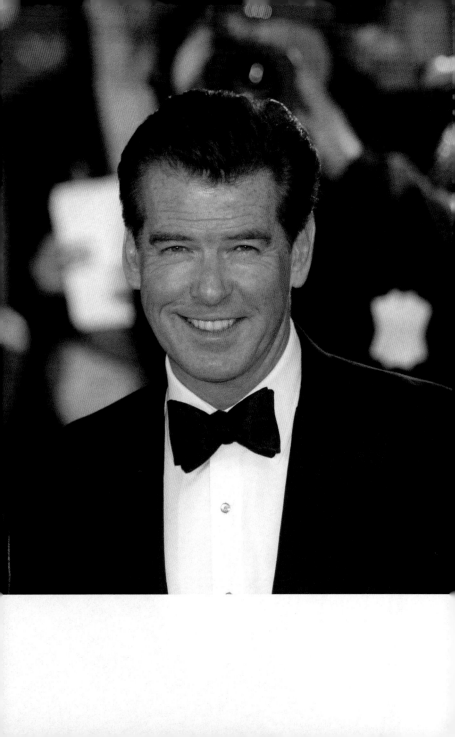

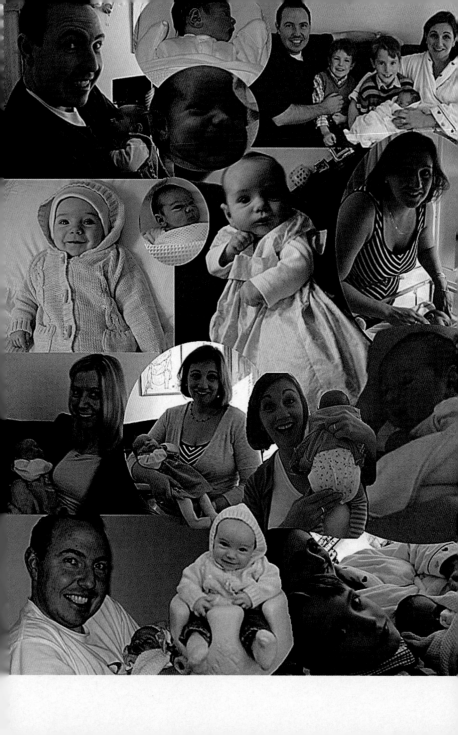

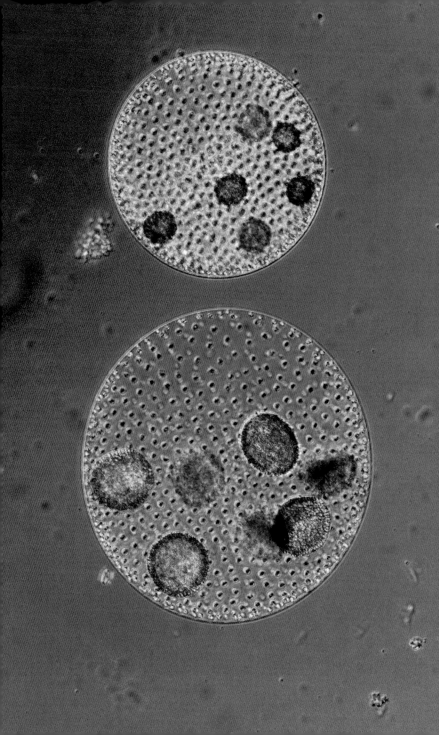

PLATE 67}

Icebergs. Such eerie beauty and elemental power that they seem to belong to another world. And what colours! Greens and blues that only icebergs produce. *Melanie McGrath, writer, London*

Ice cream. It has been proven that people who like ice cream are happier than those who don't. *Zoe Ashpole, full-time mum, Manchester*

INDIFFERENCE

Ignorance. How much don't we know? *Natasha Lombart, marketing consultant, Hertfordshire*

Illiteracy. That so many secretly illiterate adults can function and succeed undiscovered in the world. *Noreen Khan, designer, London*

Imaginary companions. According to research by the universities of Washington and Oregon, 65 per cent of children under the age of 7 have had an imaginary companion, ranging from invisible boys and girls to squirrels, panthers and elephants, and that 95 per cent of school-age children engage in impersonation. My own daughter had '11 sisters' who lived above our living room door. Wish I still had mine. *Anonymous, London*

'India', my smooth-haired fox terrier bitch. Particularly the smell of her ears. *Tom Ford, designer, New York*

Indifference. I suppose one man's wonder is another man's indifference. *Toby Glanville, photographer, London*

75

IMAGINARY COMPANIONS *Anonymous*

Infinity. *Toby, primary school pupil, London*

Instinct. How does the Canada Goose know it is time to migrate south for the winter and make the journey in a perfect V formation with all the other geese? How does the brown bear know he should start stuffing his face in preparation for his long winter hibernation? How does the tiny hummingbird know it is time to fly to Brazil for the winter? Instinct is a true marvel and, without it, many species (including humans) would be extinct. *Sally Scott, marketing director, London*

Internal clock. Waking up a minute before the alarm goes off. *Sandy Warren, mother and company director, London*

Internet. *Langlands & Bell, artists, London*

Intricacy. Detail is always good. *Ryan Ras, designer, London*

Italy. Even with its terrible bureaucracy and taxes. The beautiful view of the hills from my bedroom window. Cherry picking in May, wine tasting, risotto with truffles, cycling through the countryside with the sun on my face, a meal at Sirmione on Lake Garda with friends, dancing until dawn at La Corte degli Aranci … shall I go on? *Rosalia D'Aprano, Vicenza, Italy*

{PLATE 19}

childhood is the world of miracle and wonder; as if creation rose, bathed in the Light, out of the darkness, utterly new and fresh and astonishing. The end of childhood is when things cease to astonish us.

—

Eugène Ionesco
(1909-1994)

Jackdaws. How many times must they throw twigs down a chimney to no avail before deciding this is *not* going to be a good nesting

place? Jackdaws are supposed to be intelligent. Maybe it isn't the same pair who do all the twig-throwing? *Vanessa Mitchell, copyeditor, London*

Jamon nero. *Amy, student, London*

Japanese foot binding. *Vassilysa, jeweller, New York*

Jeans. Truly magnificent. The perfect pair can make you feel like you have a body to die for. *Claire Wilson, administrator, Lancashire*

Jelly fish. *James Wells, diving enthusiast, London*

Jesus Christ. The perfect man. A man who didn't have a bad word to say about anybody. Ever. Or even a bad thought. Even his anger was righteous. And 2000 years later we are still trying to figure out how he managed it. *Wendy Grisham, publisher, London*

ALL wonder is the effect of novelty on ignorance.
–
samuel johnson
(1709-1784)

---

*Originating in China, the ancient cruel practice of foot binding was banned by Japan in 1894 and by China in 1911.

JAPANESE FOOT BINDING *Vassilysa*

Kelly, Grace (b. 2006). My niece. Adorable and captivating, she has brought love to so many people. *Sue Nash*

Kiss.* (1) That such a fleeting touch of the lips can carry so much meaning, information and emotion, from the very first to a final sign off. The first kiss is one we should all remember, even if, like mine, it was an awkward fumbling in the school playground. I recall she ate sweets so her lips were sugared and tasty. Then there are hardcore snogs and more passionate embraces,

or the gentle kiss on the head of a newborn child; that kiss on cheek to cheek that signifies friendship and travel; to what, I hope, is a final lingering kiss from my lover before I go off to meet my maker. *John Denton, digital media executive, London* **(2)** From the Old English word *cyssan* 'to kiss,' in turn from *coss*. Kisses of all kinds are an instinctive reaction that cannot be compared to anything else. I think not many people realize nowadays how powerful this tiny, simple act can be. It brings so much happiness. Why do we not kiss more? *Luz Valencia, artist, Barcelona* **(3)** Kissing under water - the 'snorkel kiss'. *Annie Cowan,† writer/performer, London*

---

*According to the American Academy of General Dentistry, kissing helps prevent tooth decay because it stimulates the production of saliva, which in turn helps reduce the incidence of cavities.

†Annie Cowan's other wonders: 'Seeing your dad try not to cry. Seeing you mum literally piss her pants after you've eventually made her laugh in a public place. Watching an eclipse in a crop circle in Rouen with everyone wearing glasses (it looked like something out of *Close Encounters*). Words that don't sound like the thingimmejig you're talking about, but get stuck in your mind like a Eurovision song, e.g. "wibwob", a 17th-century word for a fanny.'

Kitchen cupboard.
Being given a recipe and finding that you already have all the ingredients you need. *Mo Mohsenin, promotions and sponsorship manager, London*

Klein bottle. First described in 1882 by the German mathematician Felix Klein, the Klein bottle is a non-orientable object like the Möbius strip, which has no definite inner or outer surface. It manages (almost) to be 2D, 3D and 4D at the same time. And is a great example of transforming something that ought only to be a concept into something physically real. A proof of human ingenuity. *Mark Rappolt, writer/editor, London*

{FIG. 17}

Lake Huron, Ontario. The trees on Georgian Bay. *Bryan Adams, musician, London/Toronto*

Landscapes. Beautiful landscapes – such as Banff National Park in Canada, for example – overwhelm me. I am fascinated by what lies beyond my laboratory and grateful for the ability to travel and meet people in these places. *Sue-Ying To, biomedical scientist, Brighton*

Language. The way the written word lasts for generations. All the different ways we can express our feelings and describe the world around us. *Angharad Brown, web editor, London*

PLATE 54}

Lanvin pumps. After 'renewable energy', I thought about my new Lanvin pumps. They cost a fortune, but

anything by Lanvin right now makes me feel warm and cuddly. They're Reykjavik blue satin with the same colour laces and a gun-metal leather toe-cap. They rock! *Mike Radcliffe, director, London*

Laughter. *Milly Baker, senior PR executive, London*

Launching the Great Wall of China into Orbit as a Satellite around the Moon (1969). The artwork by David Medalla. *Rebecca and Mike, designers, London*

Lava. *Harriet Quick,* journalist, London*

{PLATE 55}

Lavender fields in Grasse, Provence. *Elaine Farrance, nanny, London*

Lead house. At the bus station in Montreal, Canada. *Beth Derbyshire, artist, London*

{FIG. 18}

The few wonders of the world only exist while there are those with the sight to see them.
–
Charles de Lint
(b. 1951)

*Harriet Quick's other wonders include 'Hummingbirds, starfish, morning light and endless flowers.'

FIG. 17. LAKE HURON (TREES ON GEORGIAN BAY) *Bryan Adams*

Libraries. Free houses of imagination and knowledge. *Clare Cumberlidge, curator, London*

Life itself! It needs no explanation. *Sir Paul Smith, designer and shopkeeper, London*

Light. Because it travels in waves. *Marianne Noble, designer, London*

PLATE 12} **Light switch.** The in-line switch designed by Achille Castiglioni. A piece of modern design that actually works. It feels very expensive too, but it's actually very cheap. *Graham Mancha, furniture dealer, Hertfordshire*

Lindt chocolate balls. The delectable interiors deserve their own religion. *Melanie McGrath, writer, London*

Liverpool Football Club. The history, the passion, Dudek's double save, Riise's left foot, and just everything that Stevie G[errard] does on the pitch. *Sheila Sanders, accounts payable, Leicester*

Living. A very good friend of mine died in the 7/7 bombings, so I'm just thankful to be here. How lucky I am to be alive. Bombings happen every day, so I just enjoy life on a day-to-day basis, thanking God for allowing me to live. *Naz Begum, law student, Essex*

Locatelli's white truffle spaghetti. *Amelia Noble, art director, London*

London. (1) The view from the train crossing Blackfriars Bridge: the Gherkin, Tate Modern and St Paul's Cathedral, a lovely snapshot of modern and historic London. *Tracey Sinclair, researcher/writer, London.* (2) The walk over London Bridge is the nicest part of my commute. The view of Tower

FIG. 18. LEAD HOUSE *Beth Derbyshire*

Bridge is beautiful and changes every day. *Shamini Sriskandarajah, editorial assistant, London*

{PLATE 64}

Lost food, empty squares and party bombs. Everyday wonders of the 21st century: that in the 21st century food still falls from the hands in the act of eating it; that public squares can be so empty while aeroplanes are so full; that bombs are still for war and not for parties – a bomb is always a big surprise. *Marti Guixé, designer, Barcelona and Berlin*

Love. (1) Why does everyone want something that is so great to have, but so painful to lose? *Stacey Kilpatrick, helpdesk analyst, Leicester* **(2)** Sounds corny, but when love is true, real, honest and without limits, it is totally transformative. *Karen Garratt, artist/writer, London* **(3)** The greatest conundrum of all. I do wonder at how much it is possible to love your children (whilst they drive you mad) and how difficult it sometimes seems

to love another human adult. But that's just me. *Vanessa Andrews, marketing consultant, Putney* **(4)** I was watching comedienne Jo Brand's 'Driving Me Crazy' TV programme last week. It featured a married couple in their 90s. Their tenderness and fondness for each other was really touching. I think it is a true wonder that some people find their soulmate and get to share their whole life together. *Rita Daly, Alderholt, near Fordingbridge* **(5)** How can something be so simple and complicated at the same time? *Julia Castillo, designer, London*

Love of God. *Ashlynne Wilson, student, Sydney*

Lycra. Life *before* Lycra: {PLATE 27} itchy, saggy tights, trousers that scythed off the patella in a deep bend, lingerie that scratched and suffocated. *After* Lycra: moveable, breathable, comfortable fabric. Deep joy. *Helen Campbell, ex-banker, now scruffy art student, Marylebone, London*

LAUGHTER *Milly Baker*

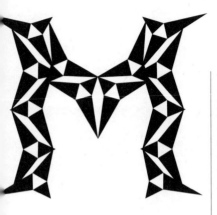

there). But then surely Cy Coleman's music and Dorothy Fields' lyrics are the real magic of *Sweet Charity* – unless you consider that without the wit and charm of writer Neil Simon, Charity would, after all, be just another rather dull 'dance hall hostess'. No, it has to be the big guy himself – Bob Fosse.† No one can beat the true original wonder that is Fosse – except, for me, sweet Charity Hope Valentine herself. Maybe she will indeed 'live hopefully ever after'. (I can't believe I'm not mentioning Stephen Sondheim... where to start? Lordie, what about Liza Minnelli and her glorious, tortured rendition of 'Maybe This Time' in Fosse's *Cabaret*? Or Judy Garland singing 'The Man Who Got Away'...) *Sandy, fan, London*

Magic mushrooms. *Jack Saunders, artist, Columbia*

{PLATE 2}   **Machu Picchu, Peru.** Not as ancient as it looks, but still amazing. Hidden by the jungle until the 20th century, this 1450s Inca city thrived for just a brief period before it was snuffed out by imperial conquerors. *Stephen Ross, marketing director, London*

{FIG. 19}   **MacLaine, Shirley (b. 1934).*** How could anything top her heart-breaking performance as Charity Hope Valentine in the 1969 classic film-version of *Sweet Charity*? Perhaps that's unfair to Gwen Verdon, who did, after all, create the role on Broadway in 1966 (the year of my birth – obviously no coincidence

---

*Born Shirley MacLean Beaty, MacLaine won an Academy Award in 1984 for her performance in the film *Terms of Endearment*. MacLaine's younger brother is actor Warren Beatty (born Henry Warren Beaty).

---

†In 1973, Bob Fosse (1927-87) won a Tony Award for *Pippin* and *Sweet Charity* on Broadway, an Academy Award for his film version of *Cabaret*, and an Emmy Award for *Liza with a 'Z'*, the first person ever to win all three of these awards in the same year. His other works as a director and choreographer include *All That Jazz*, *Damn Yankees*, *Chicago* and *Star 80*.

89

FIG. 19. SHIRLEY MACLAINE (B. 1934) IN SWEET CHARITY *Sandy*

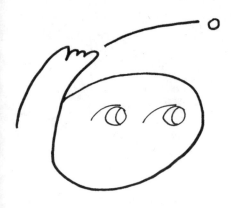

MARBLES *James and James*

Magnetic kissing dolls.
A boy and a girl dressed up in plastic Dutch costume. I had two sets when I was young and was obsessed with trying to make the two boys kiss. Of course they wouldn't: because of the magnetic charges, the boy could only be convinced to peck the girl. Fifteen years later, I met my partner Damian. We went to a market and came across the magnetic dolls of my childhood. I told him the story of what I used to do with the toys and held two of them to illustrate the point. Shockingly, the two plastic boy dolls leaned forward and gently kissed each other. How did that happen? Who had put the two opposing magnets in these dolls that finally allowed them to kiss? Was it a sign? Perhaps it was. That day we we bought the dolls and have been together ever since. *David Nicholls and Damian Foxe, journalists, London*

Mahler, Gustav (1860-1911). Symphony No.5 by Mahler is my 'Wonder of the World'. *Sir Menzies Campbell, politician, Westminster*

Make-up. Concealer, blush, lippy: all a girl needs to feel fantastic, confident and ready to face the world, looking and feeling great! *Kerry Marsh, civil servant, Manchester*

Mandela, Nelson (b.1918). {FIG. 20}
Can a person be a wonder of the world? Yes - in a simple handshake (strong and friendly) - oh, yes, the smiles and frowns seemed a 1,000 years old, and yes you couldn't find a trace of anger in his eyes - even though his loss is sometimes too much for the human race to bear - but his hellos and goodbyes brought tears to our eyes. *Bruce Weber and Nan Bush, New York*

Man-made objects. {PLATE 52}
The radiant blue of the plastic

bucket on the concrete steps. The fluorescent green bristles on the small wooden broom. The accidental scattering of hand-cut paper stars on the ground. The electric green hosepipe curled up to perfection like a snake. The yellow umbrella leaning against the yellow striped glass. The tiny bright corners left by ripped-away posters. The green rubber bands in the wooden *sake* cup. The big red apples printed on the pink cardboard box. The opaque white umbrella lit by headlights at dusk. For weeks I can find myself thinking of something I've seen. Man-made or a result of human interaction with them, these objects with their unintentionally beautiful colour and composition, blow me away. *Lucinda Noble, designer, Tokyo*

Manners. Good ones and, occasionally, bad. *Robert Ksienski, musician, London*

Mantegna, Andrea (1431–1506), painter. Apart from riding in a small boat beneath Niagra Falls, standing in front of a painting in Milan by Andrea

Mantegna touched me like none had ever before. It sang to me across the centuries about human love and suffering. I was transfixed for ages and was left weeping at the honesty and passion of the piece and its simple message. *Brian Popay, London*

Mapplethorpe's Tulips.* *Ashleigh Vinall, art director, London*

Marbles. Even cave people played marbles and they have been found in Aztec pyramids. *James and James, illustrators, London*

Marine Mammal Program.† It's only a matter of years before the US Navy train a giant squid. *Greg Lynn, architect, Venice, California*

{PLATE 24}

---

*Robert Mapplethorpe (1946–1989), photographer famous for his erotic, still-life and celebrity portraits, whose work frequently troubled religious and political conservatives in the US.

†In San Diego, the US Navy Marine Mammal Program has trained dolphins and sea lions to clear sea mines, detect divers and lost equipment. First developed in 1960 and partly declassified in the 1990s, the program has deployed its animals during wars in Vietnam and Iraq. Other animals studied by the NMMP include killer whales, elephant seals and sharks.

Nominated by the American Society of Civil Engineers, to honour the 20th century's greatest achievements in civil engineering

MODERN WONDERS

PANAMA CANAL, ISTHMUS OF PANAMA (1914)
To build the Panama Canal, more than 42,000 workers shifted enough earth to bury Manhattan Island to a depth of 3 metres. The 13.2 km-long series of locks, resevoir lakes and artificial channels, saves a journey of 8,000 miles around Cape Horn.

NORTH SEA PROTECTION WORKS, THE NETHERLANDS (1927–1963)
A 32-km-long enclosure dam was initially completed in 1930, followed over the next four decades by additional works to protect the Dutch lowlands from storm surges.

EMPIRE STATE BUILDING, NEW YORK (1931)
Built in 13 1/2 months, the Empire State Building was for 41 years the tallest skyscraper in the world (381 metres), and, until 11 September 2001, the most famous.

GOLDEN GATE BRIDGE, SAN FRANCISCO (1937)
At 2,737 metres long, the Golden Gate Bridge can withstand a nearby earthquake measuring up to 8.3 on the Richter Scale. Its two towers stand 227 metres tall, and its massive cables contain enough wire to encircle the Earth three times.

CN TOWER, TORONTO, CANADA (1976)
At 553.33 metres, the world's tallest free-standing structure, three times the height of the Seattle Space Needle.

ITAIPU DAM, PARANÁ RIVER, BRAZIL-PARAGUAY BORDER (1984)
The Itaipu Dam contains enough concrete to build five Hoover Dams and enough steel and iron to build 300 Eiffel Towers.

CHANNEL TUNNEL (1994)
31 miles long – including a 24-mile stretch 40 metres below the sea bed of the English Channel – the Tunnel links Britain with France. First conceived (notionally) as early as 1802, it took seven years to build and cost about £10 billion (80 per cent over-budget).

Marmite. *Vivian Aʃh, perʃonal aʃʃiʃtant, London*

Mastectomy. My wonder is that following a mastectomy to remove a large breast tumour and being bald from chemotherapy, I still feel feminine! *Karen Barrett, local government worker, Hudderʃfield*

Matchbox model of a 1914 Sunbeam motorcycle and side-car (from the Yesteryear series). It sits next to my laptop as I type this. Though it is No. 8 in the series, I'm pretty sure this is the first one I got in 1965, when I was five years old. I was living in Madagascar at the time, so it had (for those days) made a pretty significant trip from the Mattel/Lesney factory in Hackney. The wonder of this item is all to do with me and my past, and how a small bit of fashioned metal and plastic captures the history of a world-famous toy maker, my relationship with my offspring, and my memories of long-ago birthday presents from parents (now dead) in a country far away. *Ken Arnold, head of public programmeʃ for a truʃt, London*

Maths. Its consistency is the exception to the rule in our chaotic world. For me, maths is the source of infinite beauty: repetition, structure, order, curves. And it almost makes me believe that the whole affair was organized from beyond. *Harry Allen, deʃigner, New York*

Matterhorn, Zermatt, Switzerland. This is the wonder that keeps the stars apart. *Suʃʃan Modjtahedi, creative conʃultant, London*

Mayonnaise. An awesome example of kitchen alchemy. *Guido Vericat, architect, London*

McIntosh MC275 valve amplifier: I love the sculptural aesthetics of turntables and the agricultural beauty of valve amps, particularly this one from the 1960s. *Leʃ Wong, hi-fi dealer, London*

McQuade, Millie (b. 2006). The truly wondrous Millie McQuade, age six months. See my collage... it took me a bit of time to produce. *Marina McQuade, auditor, Leiceʃter*

{PLATE 36}

Memory. Our innate faculty for memory and

recognition - the basis for survival and evocative experience. The older you get, the more you notice it. For example: recognising a single face in a crowd of people, encountering a smell or sound, detecting meaning in a work of art or poetry. *David Noble, artist, East Sussex*

Men. Fathers, brothers, friends and lovers. We love them, we hate them, we crave them and we want to punch their lights out. And in all circumstances, at all times, we wonder one thing - what makes them tick? *Wendy Grisham, publisher, London*

{FIG. 21}

Meteorite. The one I own is 500 million years older than any rock on Earth and is the *sine qua non* of our entire world. It contains all the elements, more or less in their cosmic proportions, created from hydrogen and helium in stars that have come and gone since the birth of the Universe, until a moment 4,500 million years ago when our sun and planets were born. It is one of the most primitive forms of meteorite, called a *carbonaceous chondrite*, that

fell to Earth on 8 February 1969, near the town of Allende, Mexico. It is a thin slice (about 40 mm across) of the full two-tonne mass and consists of small white grains that were liquefied by the new born sun and then mixed into a carbon-rich matrix colder and farther from the sun. The planets formed as these small rocks slowly collected under their own self-gravity. The meteor, formed at the birth of our solar system, was never incorporated in a planet and orbited the sun until it finally collided with Earth 38 years ago. It is the substance from which Earth was built and contains the building blocks of life. From this come gold, diamonds, beauty, love and passion. *Robin Catchpole, astronomer, Cambridge*

Microbes. Invisible things that are everywhere - on us, in us and around us, ruling our behaviour and the world. Imagining the number on one eyelash is mind-blowing. Someone smart called them 'the invisible masters of the universe'. *Jane Withers, design consultant and writer, London*

{PLATE 37}

"Can a person be a wonder of the world?"

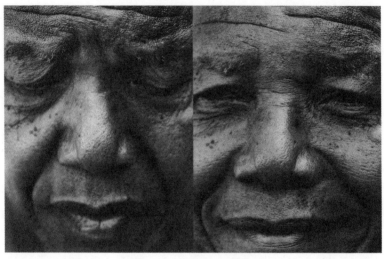

"ajes — in a simple handshake; (strong and friendly) - oh yes the smiles and frowns seemed a 1,000 years old, and yes you couldn't find a trace of anger in his eyes — even though his loss is sometimes too much for the human race to bear — but his hellos and goodbyes brought tears to our eyes."

FIG. 20. NELSON MANDELA (B. 1918) *Bruce Weber and Nan Bush*

FIG. 21. METEORITE *Robin Catchpole*

Microchip. Just as electricity was the wonder of the 20th century, the wonder of our time is the integrated circuit, or chip. Etching complex circuits on to slivers of silicon has transformed our lives by condensing improbably huge quantities of computing power. When I was a kid in the 1960s, my dad took me into 'The Computer Room' which, literally, was an enormous room filled with scarily big metal cabinets, presumably with the combined power of less than an iMac. The chip not only saved us from that, but gave us the PC, Internet, email, cellphones and other digital stuff that makes our lives easier and more enjoyable. It also - although I'm not sure that we really appreciate this yet - has freed us from the assumption that size = power. If I had to choose just one of the contemporary wonders that the chip has given us, it would be the X01, the cute little computer that promises to transform the educational prospects of needy children in the developing world.

The X01 is the brainchild of One Laptop Per Child, a non-profit organization founded by the US technologist, Nicholas Negroponte, to design, develop and manufacture a laptop computer, which is to be sold for no more than US $100 and used by the children who need it most. *Alice Rawsthorn, design writer and curator, London*

Millau Viaduct, River Tarn, France. {PLATE 14} The colossal road bridge over the River Tarn in the south of France. At 343 m (maximum height to the top of the tallest pier), it stands 43 m higher than the Eiffel Tower. Designed by Foster & Partners and costing 32,000,000 euros, it so high that the road is often above cloud level. Words can't describe it. *David Noble, artist, East Sussex*

Miller, Bode (b. 1977).* *Robert Violette, publisher, London*

---

*World champion ski racer in four disciplines and, in 2005, overall World Cup Champion. Only the fifth skier in history to win World Cup races in all five disciplines, Miller has admitted to racing while drunk, and crashes out of races more often than he finishes.

Mirrors. *Abigail Simpson, student, London*

Mixtapes. I love it when someone makes you a mixtape; a personalised collection of songs that has been carefully thought about, specifically ordered and you can't skip through the tracks. *Amy Preston, designer, London*

Model of Earth. Sadly no longer on view at the Science Museum in Munich – a truly wonderful institution. A model of the Earth about two metres in diameter that spun on its axis, set at an angle off vertical. This globe was covered in models of

objects made of materials from different parts of the world: paper toys from Japan, plastic junk from the US, metal implements from Russia and wooden things from Brazil, etc. The speed at which it spun was a bit erratic and after a while of watching it became clear why: it slowed right down as the Russian metal objects reached the top, and then raced along as their weight started downwards. Tucked away in one of the less-used staircases in this vast museum, it appeared to be an astronomy exhibit about the rotation of the Earth. Then, when I spotted the models of the objects, I thought it described the material composition of parts of the world, and maybe the dominant economies of each region. It was only as I left the exhibit that I spotted a nearby explanatory label: 'All the toys [it said] are stuck onto the globe with x glue.' It was just an elaborate piece of product advertising - and it wasn't on show when I last visited. *Ken Arnold, head of public programmes for a trust, London*

A Moment in Time (1988), by Peter Aldridge. At the V&A, an exquisitely conceived and crafted sculpture of low-ion glass shards and dichroic film. Formerly a Tutor in Ceramics and Glass at the Royal College of Art (1972–78), Aldridge has immersed himself in the highest levels of glass technology, working for many years with the glass industry in the US. Taking the iconography of the crystal as a metaphor of life, and regeneration, he has made a mesmerising object that dances responsively to your movement around it. *Eric Parry, architect, London*

wonder is the foundation of aLL phiLosophy.
—
micheL de Montaigne
(1533–1592)

{FIG. 22}

Moons. *Alison Jackson, artist, London*
Mother-love. The affiliation between mother and child, which grows every day and forms one of the strongest bonds ever known. *Rubia Link, mother, New York*

Motion sensors. *Jess Wells, designer, London*
Mountain biking. Free-wheeling down a scarily steep hill on my mountain bike. This definitely makes the effort to get up to the top worth it. *Nancy Wainscoat, public relations manager, London*
Mud. Has so many uses. *Jenny Rosbottom, working mother, Croydon*
Mudskippers. Fish that live out of water. They walk, climb trees, have tiny little elbows, big googly eyes and breathe through their skin. Could talk all day about Mudskippers; they dig tunnels by scooping mud up with their mouths and spitting it out. They have 360-degree vision and would

{PLATE 22}

even survive if they were submerged in cyanide.
I am buying two next month. *Sophie Groves, recruitment agent, Leicester*

{PLATE 32}

Museum of Jurassic Technology, Los Angeles. With the Pitt Rivers Museum in Oxford, my joint wonder of the modern world. While everyone knows the eclectic and chaotic logic of Pitt Rivers, few have been seduced by the treasures at the MJT. Where else in the world could you see, in one collection and in a building that defies the laws of space, everything you could ever need to know about Soviet Space Dogs, History of the American Mobile Home, What to Say if You Meet a Hare at Night and the decaying dice of Ricky Jay. The MJT is a *wunderkammer* in the truest sense, bewitching the viewer into spending three hours longer than he intended immersed in esoterica, and who then emerges blinking into the LA sunshine, unsure whether he has been enriched or duped, nor much caring. *Richard Strange, artist, musician, writer, adventurer, London*

Music. (1) To quote Shakespeare: 'If music be the food of love, play on' ... and on and on and on. *Haydn Galloway, student, Manchester* (2) It's universal and can express every possible emotion. *Leyla Lavelle, creative assistant, London* (3) Because it makes me smile and want to dance on the grumpy rush-hour Tube journey. *Nikki Hunter, London*

My computer. And: contact lenses, fast food, Japanese food, Chinese food, antibiotics, MRI, X-ray, DNA, skiing, electric cars, mobile phones, sunshine, hot baths, London parks, frog flippers, face cream, how to choose? *Jill Ritblat, London*

My job. Being a chef and being creative; to be able to create anything with no real boundaries is one of life's greatest wonders. Cooking is almost totally limitless and I love it. *Tom Aikens,* chef, London*

---

*Tom Aikens' other wonders are the Look 585 touring bicycle, the Pro-ject Debut/Phono SB audio system with Teac CR-H255 cd player/receiver and, lastly, the Tag Heuer 69 Monaco watch.

FIG. 22. MOONS *Alison Jackson*

Mythology. The unfamiliar and unexpected awaits us round the corner. In a world where there are few mysteries left, I embrace the myths of the past. *Johanna Bonnevier, graphic design intern, London*

My wedding day. Surrounded by family and friends helping us celebrate the happiest day of our lives. *Alison Smith, paediatric staff nurse, Southampton*

{PLATE 44}

Nano technology. *Jane Simpson, consultant, Oxford*

'LATE 68}

Natural camouflage. *Philip Jones, building inspector, London*

Newborn anything. *Sarah Sands, shop assistant, Manchester*

New York Greek Deli paper coffee cup. Even though most New Yorkers actually drink soy lattes, to the rest of the world nothing says 'New York' like a bad cup of deli coffee served in a blue-and-white paper cup. Because of its use on TV shows such as 'NYPD Blue' and 'Law and

Order', even non-New Yorkers know that this is the authentic way to drink java on the streets of Manhattan. The cup, printed in royal blue and tawny gold, features the silhouettes of three steaming cups and, hand-rendered to evoke early Greek carved letterforms, a phrase that belongs to some long-forgotten era of chirpy retail attitudes: **We Are Happy to Serve You**. On the cup's sides are illustrations of a decorative amphora, a Greek vessel, once used to transport wine or oil. And the rims are decorated with a variation of a rectilinear meander, or Greek key-pattern. Other of the city's symbols have names attached to them. Why not this? Since its post-9/11 revival, and its creator's repeated name checks, most New Yorkers are aware that the I-heart-NY-symbol was designed by Milton Glaser. But few are familiar with Leslie Buck, now an octogenarian retiree living in Delray Beach, Florida, and who designed the cup in 1963. As an employee of the Connecticut-based paper cup

FIG. 23. SIR EDMUND HILLARY SURVEYING MOUNT EVEREST, 1953 *Kenton Cool*

Kenton Cool,* mountaineer,
London and Chamonix

MY NATURAL WONDERS

THE VIEW FROM THE SUMMIT OF EVEREST {FIG. 23}
The world stretches out beneath your feet. Impossible to describe. The most moving sight after weeks of toil to get there. For the last few steps of my first summit I was alone. I looked over the world and for a few precious minutes it was mine.

BRYCE CANYON, UTAH
At sunset, when the ancient red sandstone turns a deep red – like a blood orange – as the sun dips until … poof, it's gone.

STORMS CLEARING OVER CERRO TORRE, PATAGONIA
Ice-capped granite spires piercing a brooding sky at dusk. Clouds duelling the spires, racing over them. The realisation that we are just weak little ants in the face of mother nature.

WAIST-DEEP UNTRACKED POWDER, LES GRAND MONTETS, CHAMONIX
It's always a bun-fight to get up there and make fresh tracks, but boy is it worth it. The pristine snow is like a silk sheet in front of ski tips, soft and silent. Sublime and entrancing.

THE SCOTTISH HIGHLANDS
I have spent many days battling fierce weather in attempts to climb there, fighting to get to the cliff, frozen eyelids, numb fingers, often very scared. It has it all, but you have to fight for it. Wild, untamed, truly unique.

THE FIRST BEER AFTER A HARD DAY'S CLIMB ON THE SEA CLIFFS IN PEMBROKESHIRE SITTING OUTSIDE THE PUB
… in the evening glow, resting tired arms, trying to pick the chalk out of bloodied cuticles and recounting the day. Maybe not a natural wonder, but a wondrous time, of friendship and bonding that comes from being in the hills and on the cliff face.

MY MOTHER AND FATHER
My inspiration and heroes rolled into one. I can't thank them enough.

---

*Kenton Cool (b.1973) is the first British citizen to summit Everest five times, and the first Brit to ski an 8,000 m peak.

manufacturer Sherri Cup, Buck was asked to create a design that would appeal to New York coffee shop owners and street vendors most of whom, in the 1960s, were of Greek descent. Buck recalls that it was a newspaper article about archaeological digs in the Mediterranean that inspired him. One of the unearthed vessels was an amphora and Buck says he 'felt it would be a great design and reminder of my European background as well as so many other's European backgrounds.' Buck named his cup the 'Anthora' because that was how amphora was misspelled in the article. With minimal drafting experience, Buck produced the design using the simplest of tools: pen and paper. The cup's design remains unchanged since its first introduction more than 40 years ago. In an era of re-branding fever, I salute such obstinacy on the part of its producers. This is exactly the kind of design, as essential and organic to New York's urban fabric as any building, that deserves to be preserved. *Alice Twemlow, design writer, New York*

Nicolson, Lyndsay Anne (b. 1989). She's at college doing body-work repairs on automobiles and tells me all about her little Rover Metro that she is 'pimping'. The joy on her face when she discribes in graphic detail what she has done on any given day is a wonder. *Pauline Nicolson, carer for the eldery, Coventry*

Night. That particular, occasional night when you have clean crisp bed sheets, clean favourite pyjamas and a bath, covered in moisturiser. *Stacey Wood, helpdesk adviser, Liverpool*

Novel. In book form, a novel doesn't need recharging and can withstand sand, coffee and being dropped from a height. You're holding another world in your hand. *Zoe Ashpole, full-time mum, Manchester*

Octopus. (1) For their ability to camouflage themselves with incredible results. They have a skeletonless interior and are highly intelligent – probably more intelligent than any other order of invertebrates. They have been tested with maze and problem-solving experiments, which have shown that they have both short- and long-term memory. I heard their ink has healing properties. *Ria Wilcox, artist, London.* **(2)** An octopus has no bone and therefore can fit inside any-sized hole by redistributing its flesh in an extraordinary manner. They can change colours to match their surroundings. With heightened intelligence, they elegantly wallow around the deep sea. They have one love

to which they are faithful for life, until eventually the foreplay is over and they have sex. The male dies shortly afterwards of total exhaustion whilst the female gives birth to a million eggs and then gently withers away. How wonderous is that? *Ab Rogers, designer, London*

'**OK**'. *Alan Ash Newton, retail assistant, London*

Olympic Park, Seattle, Washington. A sculpture park designed by Weiss/Manfredi Architecture, a present-day wonder, especially when it reaches maturity. *Annabelle Selldorf, architect, New York*

Omnichord. A little instrument made by Suzuki that plays chords and rhythms, invaluable for the semi-competent like myself. I've had one for decades, and written many a song with it. *Brian Eno, artist and musician, London*

Onomatopoeia. Why doesn't it sound like what it means? *Rita Lippay, geneologist, Van Buren*

Orang-utans. The most amusing, adorable, playful creatures on the planet. Seeing them in their natural

ORANG-UTANS *Jean King*

habitat in Borneo was fantastic. We must save them from extinction. *Jean King, semi-retired fashion merchandiser, London*

Orgasms. Need more time to think of one wonder – but my orgasms are pretty high on the list. *Karen Garratt, artist/writer, London*

> TO be surprised,
> to wonder,
> is to begin to
> understand.
> –
> JOSE ORTEGA Y GASSET
> (1883-1955)

Others. I wonder how many people are thinking what I'm thinking at this very moment. I wonder what pain this man opposite me on the Tube has in his life, and this woman in front of me on the bus, and the couple angry at each other in the super-market. The kids being walked to school, the laughing grandad in the park, the suited businessman on the street, the lady who gives you

tissues in the toilets of a club. We share pain, joy, wonder. We are all connected. Most of the time we don't see it or we don't want to. I wonder how we can be kinder to each other. *Jessie Brennan, artist, London*

Owls. There's something quite people-like about owls. They stand upright with a round face, intense eyes and little feathered trousers for legs. People imagine them as wise, knowledgeable characters, but they probably don't have a clue. *Corinne Quin, designer, London*

Oxygen. *Bella Anomie, student, London*

{PLATE 39}

OTHERS *Jessie Brennan*

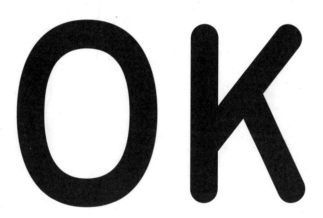

OK *Alan Ash Newton*

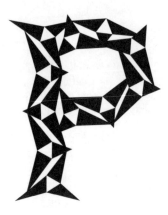

Pacific Ocean. Its colour, expanse, unfathomable force, its place in the histories of people, explorers, the arts. For those who have never lived by the Pacific, it lives in their imaginations. *Suzanne Cotter, curator, Oxford*

Pain relief. From illness or injury and in any form. *Lawrence Box, writer, Boston*

Palm (hearts of). A salad of palm hearts, freshly cut for you and in front of you in the heart of the Amazonian rainforest in Brazil. *Marie-Agnès Gillot, dancer, Paris*

Paper (white sheet of). I can fold it, draw or write on it. A luminous and pure space, an open 'door'. It gives me the freedom to do what I feel like doing, the moment I want to. *Raphaelle Pinoncél, graphic designer, Arles*

Paper clip. *Hannah Lanestow, manager, London*

Parrot (smartest ever). {PLATE 6}
Sasha speaks and understands everything. He is like a little human! He lives in Moscow with my family and has been in the local papers twice. Sasha is a true wonder that deserves to be shown to the world. *Emilia Bairamova, fashion student, London*

Parton, Dolly (b. 1946). {PLATE 66}
Such a big voice from someone so small! *Serena Gates, actress, Los Angeles*

Patriarchal monarchies. *Richard Bartlett, company director, Suffolk*

Pazyrk Carpet, Hermitage Museum, St Petersburg, Russia. The earliest nearly intact carpet yet found. It dates from the fifth century BCE and was discovered in 1949 preserved in ice high in the Altai Mountains of central Asia. Knotted carpets made by nomadic weavers are, to me, the epitome of a fundamental human need to create by artifice an ordered framework to uplift (psychologically and physically) the human spirit, surrounded as it is by a natural or man-made

wilderness. The spinning, dyeing, loom preparation, knotting and finishing of a carpet is an undertaking of the highest sophistication carried out with the simplest of means. It is capable of enabling the reverie and wonder of a world apart. *Eric Parry, architect, London*

Peace on earth. *Ben Milburn, primary school teacher, London*

Penguins. *Steve Watson, primary school teacher, London*

Penny coin. For me the 1 p coin represents the expression 'the penny dropped'. It means that (finally) you have understood

something, you have made the connection. The image is of a stuck slot machine; you put in your penny but nothing happens, and you have to thump the machine and rattle it until the penny drops and out pops your ticket, your chocolate bar, whatever. Not to forget the bonus question 'Would a penny dropped from the Empire State Building kill someone on the ground?' *Philip Colbert, designer, London*

Peonies. The big, fat, white, tree peony in my garden. *Jasper Conran,* designer, London*

Pepper mill. On the face of it, unless you happen to be a designer, you might not notice this particular pepper grinder. It's discrete in an industrial kind of way, and, despite its modern appearance, has been with us for almost 45 years. It was designed by Carlo Mazzeri and Anselmo Vitale for Alessi, the Italian maker of table and kitchenware. I happened to

---

*Jasper Conran's other wonders: 'Billie Holiday, the later years; Arthur Devis' interior portraits; Mark Rothko's paintings ... just because.'

notice one in a household goods shop in Milan many years ago, and I've been using it ever since. It is in every respect the perfect blend of industrial technique, refined function and charming companion. In fact the more I use it, the more I am aware of how good it is, and the more respect I have for this modest utensil. *Jasper Morrison, designer, London/Paris*

Perfectly heated sauna, followed by a dip in the sea. *Mia Ruulio, events director, London*

{FIG. 24}

Periodic Table. *Julia Bass, student, London*

PLATE 30}

Petra, Jordan. (1) Nothing really prepared me for how breathtaking this 2,000-year-old-plus site is, especially its little monastery. A lost city until 1812 - plus I'm a big fan of Indiana Jones. *Jeremy Tracy, estate agent, London* (2) Overwhelming. It is untouched. You can walk and walk and escape civilisation, go back in time and live in history. It's important today for us to be reminded to take time to reflect on human culture. *Imad Mouasher, businessman, Jordan*

Pheromones.* *Laurence Boulet, communications director, Lausanne*

Pi. 3.14159... This number corresponds with everything in nature and beauty. Wowzer! *Ria Wilcox, artist, London*

Pie plate (1960s). By Benjamin W. Owen (1904-1983), of Seagrove ('Jugtown' in regional parlance), North Carolina.

---

*It is believed (but unproven) that pheromones can be detected by humans (and snakes, mice and elephants) who possess Jacobson's Organ, a small pit in the nasal septum that is the vestige of a vomeronasal organ.

GROUP	1A	2A	3B	4B	5B	6B	7B
PERIOD	ALKALI	ALKALINE	← TRANSITION ME				
1	1 H						
2	3 Li	4 Be					
3	11 Na	12 Mg					
4	19 K	20 Ca	21 Sc	22 Ti	23 V	24 Cr	25 Mn
5	37 Rb	38 Sr	39 Y	40 Zr	41 Nb	42 Mo	43 Tc
6	55 Cs	56 Ba	57 La	72 Hf	73 Ta	74 W	75 Re
7	87 Fr	88 Ra	89 Ac				

58 Ce	59 Pr	60 Nd
90 Th	91 Pa	92 U

1 H

FIG. 24. PERIODIC TABLE *Julia Bass*

	1B	2B	3A	4A	5A	6A	7A	0
→	NOBLE							
								2
			5 B	6 C	7 N	8 O	9 F	10 Ne
			13 Al	14 Si	15 P	16 S	17 Cl	18 Ar
28 Ni	29 Cu	30 Zn	31 Ga	32 Ge	33 As	34 Se	35 Br	36 Kr
46 Pd	47 Ag	48 Cd	49 In	50 Sn	51 Sb	52 Te	53 I	54 Xe
78 Pt	79 Au	80 Hg	81 Ti	82 Pb	83 Bi	84 Po	85 At	86 Rn

63 Eu	64 Gd	65 Tb	66 Dy	67 Ho	68 Er	69 Tm	70 Yb	71 Lu

85 Am	86 Cm	87 Bk	88 Cf	99 Es	100 Fm	101 Md	102 No	103 Lr

FIG. 25. PROPELLER: THE NOURMAHAL, KEIL, GERMANY, 1928
James Dyson

PIGEON CHICK

For decades I have adored North Carolina pottery for its rustic purity and pre-Minimalist essentialism. Early 20th-century potters such as Mr Owen benefited from visits by Northerners, fresh with the ideas of the Arts & Crafts movement. Only recently did I learn that these cultural missionaries settled near Pittsboro to create a sophisticated industry with local potters, deliberately reviving early American, Chinese and Japanese porcelain styles – for export up North! Mr Owen even visited the Metropolitan Museum, and his designs – from a state that prides itself on being 'hog capital of the world' – are anything but naïve. I haven't lived in North Carolina for some 25 years, and had created an idea of its quaint authenticity that is mistakenly folkloristic. As I trundle onwards in life, it is the simple things which most often cause me to pause. *Cornelia Lauf, writer and curator, Italy*

▶LATE 56} **Pigeon chick**. Have you ever seen one? *Ben Ryan, Berkshire*

PITT RIVERS MUSEUM

Pinnacles National Park, Western Australia. It's like a set from a sci-fi film. Quiet and peaceful – you feel so alone. Some rock formations look almost human. How did it come to be like this? They are over 80,000 years old. *Jade King, staff nurse, Bristol*

Pitt Rivers Museum, Oxford. Anthropological gems from all over the world here are unusually displayed typologically, grouped by form or purpose rather than by geographical or cultural origin. Lucky talismens to voodoo dolls to hair combs, all with tiny typed-out labels based on the collection of Lt-General Augustus Henry Lane Fox Pitt Rivers (1827-1900), displaying a wide variety of practical, sometimes humorous and superstitious solutions to the problems of life. Packed with exhibits that are not necessarily considered valuable or beautiful, nor usually treasured or preserved, this space and its contents reveal how different peoples have lived and thought. *Lyndsay Milne, creative director and stylist, London*

FIG. 26. MARCEL PROUST (1871-1922) *George McKenzie*

Pizza. Not the American deep-pan variety, but the thin ones in Italy with tomato sauce and mozzarella topping, crispy-baked in a hot wood-burning oven. *Richard Santi, estate agent, Chorley*

Plug (electrical). The forgotten classic and generic British electrical plug. Everyone owns at least one, and they are the lifeline for any domestic enviroment and appliance. *Jordan Dalladay-Simpson, design student, London*

Poetry-in-motion. Whatever the specifics, any of them'll do: a world-class boxer, a good film; could be this, that, something else. *Rebecca and Mike, designers, London*

Polar Bear (Isle of Wight). I can walk from my house to Southbourne Overcliff, in Dorset, and see the 'polar bear' in the natural rock formation on the cliffs of the Isle of Wight. It always makes me smile. *Jill Bamford, mother, Bournemouth*

Polaroid photographs. (1) To see an image appear before your eyes in a matter of seconds and preserve a

memory forever. *Amy Preston, designer, London* (2) A destroyed Polaroid that I found on the street about eight years ago. *Beth Derbyshire, artist, London*

Polly Pocket. Plastic toys {PLATE 65} that open, swivel and fold to reveal intricate pink and blue landscapes. They have the beauty of Fabergé eggs and the democracy of cheapness. If only all design could be so ingeniously utopian. *Sam Jacob, architect and designer, London*

Polyester trouser suit. {PLATE 48} The kind my mother wore in the 1970s. *David Cross, veterinarian, Surrey*

Porridge. I wake up, I think it's Friday, but it's Saturday. I make coffee and porridge and my husband and I eat it in bed. *Sharon Maes, travel agent, London*

Postal service. In the old days, the wonder of a system of communication that reaches us all. *Clare Cumberlidge, curator, London*

Postcards, handwriting and courtship. I used to be a big letter-writer, but now I strain to scrawl more than a few lines. I am also a flea

market girl, and I adore the early 20th-century love-letter postcards I find in Paris. Anticipation, showmanship and romance! *Jess Tully, marketing director and creative, London*

Pranayama breathing. Breath slowed down and controlled – the most worthwhile thing that I have taken away from my yoga practice. Imagine breathing through your next challenge – take a few deep breaths and focus. *Justine de Luce, estate agent, Toronto*

Presents. What difference did it make to people's lives in Africa when I gave a present to someone there for Christmas? Will that person be happy? *Cara Louise Cassidy, secondary school pupil, London*

Printing photographs in a darkroom. Watching an image appear in a developer bath and talking to the person you see there, the person that you photographed. Caressing the

paper, soft as velvet. Bare hands, no gloves. Enjoying the red light as much as sunlight. *Anne Deniau, Paris*

Propeller. Superseding {FIG. 25} the sail and paddle wheel, the propeller corkscrews through air and water with speed and elegance. Beautiful in wood, bronze or today's carbon fibre. *James Dyson, inventor, London*

Proust, Marcel (1871–1922). {FIG. 26} *George McKenzie, baker, Salisbury*

Pullman, Phillip (b.1946). Author of the fantasy trilogy *His Dark Materials*, consisting of the novels *Northern Lights*, *The Subtle Knife* and *The Amber Spyglass*. *Jess Wells, designer, London*

Pumpkin soup. No one's pumpkin soup tastes as good as my mum's. *Jessica Graham, events co-ordinator, London*

Purdie, Bernard (b.1939). 'Pretty' Bernard Purdie's half-time shuffle. *Robert Violette, publisher, London*

??????????????????????????????????????
??????????????????????????????????????
??????????????????????????????????????
??????????????????????????????????????
??????????????????????????????????????
??????????????????????????????????????
??????????????????????????????????????
??????????????????????????????????????
??????????????????????????????????????
??????????????????????????????????????
??????????????????????????????????????
??????????????????????????????????????
??????????????????????????????????????
??????????????????????????????????????
??????????????????????????????????????
??????????????????????????????????????
??????????????????????????????????????
??????????????????????????????????????
??????????????????????????????????????
??????????????????????????????????????
??????????????????????????????????????
??????????????????????????????????????
??????????????????????????????????????
??????????????????????????????????????
??????????????????????????????????????
??????????????????????????????????????
??????????????????????????????????????
??????????????????????????????????????
??????????????????????????????????????
?????????????????????????

Anonymous

Questions. Why is it
that people don't ask more of
them??????????????????????????????
??????????????????????????????????????
??????????????????????????????????????
??????????????????????????????????????
??????????????????????????????????????
??????????????????????????????????????
??????????????????????????????????????
??????????????????????????????????????
??????????????????????????????????????
??????????????????????????????????????
??????????????????????????????????????
??????????????????????????????????????
??????????????????????????????????????
??????????????????????????????????????
??????????????????????????????????????
??????????????????????????????????????
??????????????????????????????????????
??????????????????????????????????????
??????????????????????????????????????
??????????????????????????????????????
??????????????????????????????????????
??????????????????????????????????????

Quiet times. Rare in this 21st century, but a gift when it happens. *Trudy Lister, head of sales promotions, London*

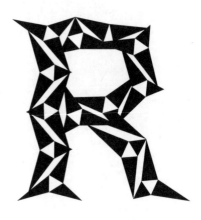

Radio waves. Waves and bandwidth: somehow music is playing in one place and can travel through the air silently and play in another. How exactly does it get there? *Kate Wilson, media consultant, Harpenden*

Rainbows. Why can't you point at them? Is there really a pot of gold at the end, and if so, where is the end and why can't anybody find it? *Deborah Traheam, Leceister*

Rainy days with duvets. Followed closely by sleeping on the beach with the sun rays on your face. *Julie Hodder, marketing manager, Cornwall*

Red. The iconic colour of the city where I live, London. While I don't dress much in red - and I know someone who only wears red - the red items I do have in my wardrobe are special. My daughter's name is Scarlet, and I yearned for a son just so that I could call him Red. Instead, I am blessed with three daughters. 'Red' Evans - sounds like a fighter pilot, or an adventurer. My football team, Arsenal, wear red, and my favourite Charles Eames chair looks even better in red. *Ben Evans, design festival director, London*

Regeneration of limbs. How do lizards grow back their tails after they are chopped off? Why we can't regrow limbs that way. (I also wonder how some really beautiful people can be really ugly.) *Lisa Simpson, researcher, London*

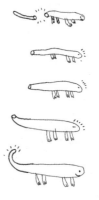

Renewable energy.
It staggers me in a world diseased with potentially catastrophic climate change that we are not making the majority of our energy through wind, sun, water, etc. We still drill for oil, mine for coal, which strikes me as madness when the Earth's renewable energy is free and so beautiful. When I drive to my house in Wiltshire, in our fuel-efficient Audi, my heart soars when I reach Reading and see a huge wind turbine with beautiful, aerodynamic blades being powered by *free* wind. Truly wonderful! *Mike Radcliffe, director, London*

Riding school in Vienna. Housed in the Winter Riding School (1735) designed by Josef Emanuel Fischer von Erlach, this is the only institution in the world that has practised for over 430 years and continues to cultivate classical equitation in the Renaissance tradition of the *haute école*. The objective of classical equitation is to study the way the horse naturally moves and to cultivate the highest levels of *haute école* elegance the

horse is capable of through systematic training. The result creates an unparalleled harmony between rider and horse. *Paul Heber-Percy and Simon Moretti, artist-curators, Paris*

Rigby. My son says and does things just like me and my mother and we wonder 'How did he *know* to do that!' *Nadja Swarovski, company vice president, London*

Right-handed people. Right-handed people live (on average) nine years longer than left-handed people. *Sophie Groves, recruitment agent, Leicester*

Ring of Brodgar, Orkney. Predates Stonehenge and is a remarkable, mystical, spiritual place. *Helen Blackburn, Salvation Army manager, Rosewell*

Roden Crater. Artist James Turrell's Roden Crater in Arizona, an amazing place that will be a wonder for the generations to come in future millennia, much like the pyramids of Giza or even Stonehenge. *Dominic Palfreyman, London*

Romance. Bus-stop romance in particular.

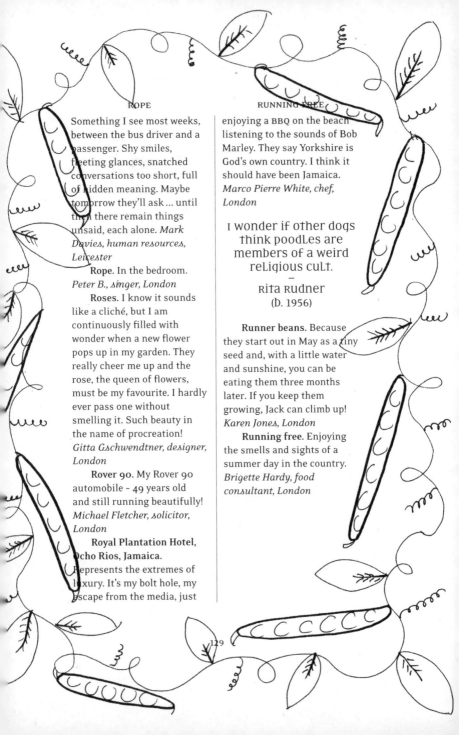

Something I see most weeks, between the bus driver and a passenger. Shy smiles, fleeting glances, snatched conversations too short, full of hidden meaning. Maybe tomorrow they'll ask ... until then there remain things unsaid, each alone. *Mark Davies, human resources, Leicester*

Rope. In the bedroom. *Peter B., singer, London*

Roses. I know it sounds like a cliché, but I am continuously filled with wonder when a new flower pops up in my garden. They really cheer me up and the rose, the queen of flowers, must be my favourite. I hardly ever pass one without smelling it. Such beauty in the name of procreation! *Gitta Gschwendtner, designer, London*

Rover 90. My Rover 90 automobile - 49 years old and still running beautifully! *Michael Fletcher, solicitor, London*

Royal Plantation Hotel, Ocho Rios, Jamaica. Represents the extremes of luxury. It's my bolt hole, my escape from the media, just

enjoying a BBQ on the beach listening to the sounds of Bob Marley. They say Yorkshire is God's own country. I think it should have been Jamaica. *Marco Pierre White, chef, London*

> I wonder if other dogs think poodles are members of a weird religious cult.
> –
> Rita Rudner
> (b. 1956)

Runner beans. Because they start out in May as a tiny seed and, with a little water and sunshine, you can be eating them three months later. If you keep them growing, Jack can climb up! *Karen Jones, London*

Running free. Enjoying the smells and sights of a summer day in the country. *Brigette Hardy, food consultant, London*

RADIO WAVES *Kate Wilson*

{FIG. 28}

the bedouin travellers traverse the high sand dunes of Arabia. This, produced by the humblest of artisans, represents the finest elements of good design: simple to execute, practical to produce and totally functional. *Phillip Nutt, ,shoe designer, Toronto*

Sant'Ivo alla Sapienza, Rome. The church built from 1642 to 1660 by the architect Francesco Borromini (1599-1667), and especially its spiral cupola. *Cornelia Lauf, writer and curator, Italy*

{PLATE 34}

Sacrifice. People like Martin Luther King who give everything of themselves for others. *Joe Wilton, London*

Salter, James (b. 1925). Read the *The Light Years*. *Jenny Kerr, gallerist, London*

Sand. How soft it is in Egypt. *Giulia, primary ,school pupil, London*

Sandals (from Yemen). My most treasured collectable is a pair of antique Yemeni sandals. My MD daughter brought them back as a gift for me after a stint in Yemen on behalf of the United Nations studying vaccination procedures. The sandals are very basic handmade leather uppers, laminated together with crude nails, but on the bottom of the sole are metal cleated strips with the functional purpose of helping

Satellite navigation. Where would I be without it? *Susan Caria, O,sterly*

Saying 'Thank you'. *Ro,sanna Banke,s, accountant, London*

Scale. Things that are vastly bigger or smaller than

me: things under a
microscope, galaxies, stars.
Something I can't really get
my head around. *Ryan Ras,
designer, London*

Scent of a garden. After
a light shower of rain: clean,
fresh and new. *Gill Abrahams,
quality systems co-ordinator,
Kings Lynn*

> Never say there is
> nothing beautiful in
> the world any more.
> There is always
> something to make
> you wonder.
> —
> Albert Schweitzer
> (1875-1965)

{FIG. 27}   **Sea.** (1) Free for all to
enjoy. Lasting memories.
Calm and peaceful, wild and
forever flowing, filled with
wonders. *Sarah Whittington,
full-time mum, eBay seller
and occasional office
secretary for a friend,
Gravesend.* (2) Soothes my
soul when the storm is in
my heart; the waves wash
the darkness away and leave
my mind completely
refreshed. *Valerie Westom,
housewife, Farnborough* (3)
Immense, unpredictable,

mysterious and stunning.
I grew up a stone's throw
from the shore and swim
in the sea every day in
summer. Chlorinated indoor
pools just don't compare!
*Rosie Baker, cover supervisor,
Manchester*

Sea horses. The only
species that I know of where
the male becomes pregnant.
*Debbie Roberts, helpdesk
administrator, Leicester*

Seed pod (giant). All seed
pods are wondrous – not least
because they are curious and
particularised vessels that
have evolved over time to
protect and disseminate seed.
In my mind's eye, this colossal
star-shaped pod comes from
a tree whose canopy must
surely scrape the sky.
*Todd Longstaffe-Gowan,
landscape designer, London*

Seger, Pete (b. 1919).
Because that glorious cracked
treble voice and that battered
banjo are the sound of the
generation that believed they
could change the world. We
shall overcome! It has to be
true. *Judith Evans,
Pontypridd, Wales*

Serengeti migration.   {PLATE 47}
Stan Goodman, Finchley

FIG. 27. SEA *Sarah Whittington, Valerie Westom, Roʃie Baker*

Scrambled Eggs with Sea Urchins

Serves 4. Why is it we don't make the most of our native seafood? OK we eat prawns, which are more often than not imported. And there's those crabsticks and prawn shapes, which sit in the cabinets of most seafood stalls in seaside towns. But when it comes to the real stuff we tend to be a little shy and reserved, unlike our friends across the water.

A few years back I stayed with a mate in Caherdaniel, County Kerry. On an unsuccessful day of fishing, I couldn't help but notice the sea urchin shells washed up amongst the rocks.

So I asked the guys from a diving school near us in this tiny harbour if they would mind grabbing us some sea urchins on their next dive. They gave us that mad tourist look and asked what we were going to do with them. When I told them we were hoping to serve them as a starter for dinner they thought we were totally nuts and didn't even contemplate the eating qualities of this rare local delicacy that they had obviously been ignoring for years.

To check that the waters were not polluted nor the Irish sea urchins a poisonous species, whilst they were diving I got straight on the phone to a couple Irish chef friends and Richard Corrigan confirmed that the local sea urchins were just fine to eat and the locals don't touch them. The dive was successful and they got us a couple of carrier bags full and wouldn't accept any payment, so that was our starter sorted.

Back at the house we got cleaning the sea urchins of their spines and cutting them in half with a pair of scissors to reveal the delicious orange interiors. We ate them as a starter just raw with a teaspoon and a squeeze of lemon juice, then the following morning we used what was left. I scrambled some local farm-fresh eggs with some butter and a little cream and just folded the orange sea urchin flesh into them at the last minute and served them back in their warmed shells.

I like to make the most of the rare pleasures in life, especially when they are free and local. Your local fishmonger may well not have sea urchins on his slab but will more than likely be able to get hold of some with advance warning.

Mark Hix, chef, London

4 large fresh sea urchins
60 g butter
8 medium free range eggs, beaten
salt and freshly ground white pepper
2-3 tablespoons double cream

Wearing a sturdy pair of gloves and, using a kitchen knife, scrape away all the spines from the sea urchins and give the urchins a good wash.

With a pair of scissors, make a hole just above the middle line of the sea urchin and carefully snip around so you have two halves. One half will be empty and the other will have orange eggs in segments.

With a teaspoon, carefully remove just the orange eggs and put them into a bowl.

Discard the rest of the sea urchin from inside the shells and give the shells a good wash and scrub.

Put the shells into a saucepan, cover with water, bring to the boil and simmer for a couple of minutes to sterilize them.

Drain and give them a final wash, removing any membrane, then dry them off.

Melt the butter in a pan, add the beaten eggs, season and cook over a low heat, stirring, until the eggs begin to set.

Stir in the double cream and cook for another 30 seconds. Stir in the sea urchin eggs, remove from the heat and spoon into the warmed shells.

Serve immediately.

Serpent (iron). From Burkina Faso, West Africa. For centuries these serpents have been placed at the doors of houses to protect the inhabitants from ghosts and demons. They are still being made today. The blacksmiths can't compete with cheap cooking pots and tools bought in from China. However, nobody imports these beautiful serpents. Therefore the blacksmiths' work has been reduced to making only these. Only the mystical aspects of the profession remain. *Clemens Weisshaar, designer, Munich/Stockholm*

Sex to music. No need to explain why. *Caroline*

Shack. On the A1065 road at Swaffham, Norfolk. This wonder, near a pig farm, always arrests my attention despite, or perhaps because of, its woeful condition and its new and ever-changing dissemblage. *Charlie de Bono, architect, London*

Shakespeare, William (1564-1616). *Andrea Sharp, musician, London*

Shoelaces. Look down at your shoes, laced with a bow. You may be the queen, a

dustman or a hollywood star, but you all got a bow. *Paul Trembath, train driver, Par (Cornwall)*

Shoes. As a young girl I used to place my newly acquired shoes at my bedside and, before falling asleep, gaze adoringly at them. Fashion starts from the feet up and can make you feel like Cinderella! *Jane Caselli, shoe designer, Wellingborough*

Sigh. The small sigh people make just as they fall asleep. *Vicky Henderson, fabric buyer, London*

Simple pleasures. Often overlooked in the pursuit of more exotic & extravagant desires: a bacon sarnie, a cup of tea, a hug. *Kirsten Elliott, researcher, London*

Sitting. In my garden early on a summer's morning, enjoying the perfect cup of tea and hearing nothing but birdsong. *Angela Moore, information officer, Telford*

Skin. The wonderful pleasure of touching another's skin; a baby's cheek, your partner's thigh, a bull terrier's belly. But most wonderfully that soft moist skin on a horse's upper lip (I'm not a great horse lover, just that bit amazes me). *Tim Molloy, creative director, London*

Sleep. (1) What is the magic of the ordinariness of a good night's sleep? *Amelia Noble, art director, London.* (2) Sleeping under the stars in wild Africa hearing the hyenas and lions roar. *Mia Ruulio, events director, London*

Sleep paralysis.* Pretty damn weird and wondrous. *Ria Wilcox, artist, London* {PLATE 62}

Smiles. (1) The ones on my grandchildren's faces when they see me. *A. Munnoch, financial adviser, Falkirk* (2) The most contagious and universally understood act of emotion in our world. *Konnie Papadamou, legal assistant, Colchester* (3) On my dogs' faces when I return home from a challenging day at work. Bliss! *Halinka Rands, local government finance manager, Chesham*

Smoking. Worthless and wonderful. *Amelia Noble, art director, London*

Snoopy. My wonder of the world is Snoopy - because he's Snoopy! *Giles Deacon, designer, London* {PLATE 26}

Snowflake. The child in me still gasps at the disturbing fact that no two snowflakes are ever the same. *Georgina Godley, creative director, London* {PLATE 60}

---

*Conscious awareness of temporary paralysis of the body just before falling asleep or after waking up, sometimes accompanied by hallucinations and lucid dreams, as evidently depicted in *The Nightmare* (1781) by Henry Fuseli.

FIG. 28. SACRIFICE: MARTIN LUTHER KING (1929-1968) *Joe Wilton*

Son. My son. I can't believe I made him! *Zoe Manzi, editor, London*

wisdom begins
in wonder.
—
socrates
(C. 470–399 BCE)

{PLATE 51}
Soprano, Tony.* Tony, Tony, Tony. *Frith Kerr, art director, London*

Sound. How it travels. *Sam Gisby, primary school pupil, Harpenden*

PLATE 33}
Space-girl. A lonely space-girl stranded on a distant planet. Her name is Priscilla Ray. *Chris Petersen, photographer, Seattle*

Sparklers. You can write your with them name and it stays in your eyes for a while. No matter how old you are they're always very fun. *Corinne Quin, designer, London*

Spiders' webs. Because no one teaches them how to do it. *Alexandra Violette, primary school pupil, London*

'Spinney'. My roly-poly kitty, lives the good life off

*As played by actor James Gandolfini in the HBO series 'The Sopranos'.

of others. She is incredibly moody, but with her strangely beautiful face she always gets her way. *Karen Wong, interactive designer, London*

Spinning wheel. My sister brought mine over from New Zealand, an inheritance from my grandmother and about 30 years old. With the arrival of this spinning wheel, came a flood of personal knowledge - things I knew about spinning that just seemed to be already there (useful things, like how to use it and what to do when things snap). I spent many childhood holidays at my grandparents' farm in the country. In the evening they spun wool and, of course, we got involved spinning wool as well. (There were very few alternatives and TV back then consisted

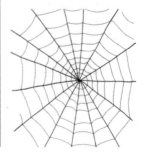

of just the News and
'Coronation Street'.) Since
the wheel has been here, in
the long dark winter evenings
I have been spinning and
finding it therapeutic and
relaxing - the rhythm and
sound of the wheel, which has
no electronic mechanism and
is of very simple construction.
Clive, headteacher, London

Spoons. My mum's
wooden spoons. These lovely,
simple tools represent my
mother's delicious, skilful,
wonderful cooking. *Susan
Gathercole, reporter,
Caernarfon*

Squirrels. Seeing them
run around campus makes me
happy. *Elin Bennett, student*

**St Basil's, Red Square,
Moscow.** One of the strangest
public squares in the world,
with the Kremlin looming on
one side, St Basil's onion
domes bulging, and Lenin's
body lying waxy in his tomb.
*Richard Jones, cabinet maker,
Tavistock*

St Ives, Cambridgeshire.
My little haven of tranquillity
and fun, fun, fun during the
Easter holidays. *Georgina
Jones, student, Upminster,
Essex*

Static shock. Startling,
comical and incredible all at
the same time. A link with the
spectacular energies of the
world, which we cannot see.
*Claire Evans, desk assistant,
St Albans*

Stefani, Gwen (b. 1969).   {PLATE 15
Woo hoo! *Emma Rich,
super-hot female, Surrey*

Stiletto heels. The x-ray
image of a stiletto by Hugh
Turvey, in the spirit of a
deformed pickled Chinese
foot I once saw in the
ethnographical museum in
Paris. A marvel it was that
women should ever have
gone to such lengths. It is a
constant wonder to me that
in 2007 women still wear a

stiletto heel, myself included. *Georgina Godley, creative director, London*

Strangers. They can be the kindest people you'll ever meet. *Jon Gisby, new media executive, Harpenden*

Suffolk Punch horse. The oldest breed of draught horse in England. I can only gaze at its perfect, robust form in wonder. *Rose English, artist, London*

{PLATE 11}   **Sun.** (1) Those golden rays brighten my days. *Sharon Clarke, teacher, Cambridge* (2) It's a wonder how different it makes things seem. *Faye Wyse, secretary, London* (3) That the sun always rises. *Elisabeth Walker, Dulwich*

Sunday roast. *Jane McAndrews, solicitor, London*

Survival. Surviving breast cancer and seeing my children reach adulthood. *Patricia Conoboy, retired administrator, Manchester*

Swearing. *Irene Simpson, receptionist, London*

{PLATE 8}   **Swingball.** There is something weird about Swingball. You whack the tennis ball (with one of those odd yellow plastic bats, of course) and instead of it

flying off in a straight line, it swings around till it whacks you in the back of the head. It turns tennis from a rectangular to a circular plan - from something that works backwards and forwards to something that goes round and round. It's like crossing a tennis court with a running track. Or looking at a straight line through a fish eye lens. Of course, it's really disappointing when the string gets tangled up and its orbital geometry collapses. *Sam Jacob, architect and designer, London*

Swiss army knife. The most useful thing known to mankind! *Jonathan Barclay, London*

Sydney Opera House. A modern day icon and wonder of the world. It stands for all things Australian and reminds me of one of my

favourite cities. *Irene Allan, marketing manager, Glasgow*

Symmetry in nature. Orchids, snowflakes, butterflies - all symmetrical, all   beautiful. The logic and simplicity of beauty are crystallised by these examples: maths + nature = wonder. *Lucy Willis, press officer, London*

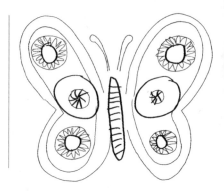

Talent. (1) The kind that takes your breath away. Bach, Mozart, Picasso or Donald Trump - a talent to do a specific thing, even to make people smile, feel comfortable. Or even a talent gone awry, like a safecracker. I'm in awe of how they do these things... Caruso, Fred Astaire, Cirque de Soleil artists ... When you think of how many people are uniquely talented in different ways, you can go on and on... Hemingway, Lloyd Wright, Pele. Yet *everyone* seems to have a talent, something they do that's a little more special than anyone else. You can't run out of people, and you can't run out of talents. *Beatrice Violette, grand-mother, Hampton* (2) Seeing someone who is the best in the world at what they do, and

has dedicated their life to it. Doesn't really matter what it is (though in my case likely to include obscure French organists improvising live). *Jon Gisby, new media executive, Harpenden*

Tancho koi carp. With a single red spot on its head, the image of the Japanese flag. They range in price from hundreds to thousands of pounds and are simply beautiful! *Leyla Lavelle, creative assistant, London*

Tarmac. Invented by accident when a barrel of tar fell of the back of a wagon and was mopped up with ash. Tarmac is practical, mendable and extendable in that it reflects a world where everything breaks, is in the wrong place and is the wrong size. But it does other things too: it makes a kind of

abstracted ground, like
a new crust to the earth.
Formed out of the leftovers
of refined crude oil, there is
something cyclic about stuff
that was once on the surface
being sucked out of the
ground and reapplied.
The Situationists said that
beneath the pavement was the
beach. Reality is much more
exotic. *Sam Jacob, architect
and designer, London*

Tarot Garden (1998) by
Niki de Saint Phalle (b. 1930).
In Tuscany, a place of sensual
textures, reflections and
voluptuous forms. *Ab Rogers,
designer, London*

Tastebuds. Some of us are
lucky enough to be able to eat
what we want, when we want.
We should take advantage
of that! Our tastebuds want
us to! Personally I like to
indulge and treat my darling

tastebuds to as many
wonderful experiences that
I possibly can. They deserve
it for the joy they bring me
every day. *Rosie Culverhouse,
former private chef, London*

Tatton Park, Cheshire.
The gardens are beautiful,
whatever time of year we
visit. *Zoe Ashpole, full-time
mum, Manchester*

Teaching. It's an amazing
feeling when you teach
children how to read, when
finally, after lots of practice
and repetition, they manage
to put together a three-letter
word for the first time. They
are so happy and proud and
it is a privilege to be part of
that moment. *Vesna Merzdan,
primary school teacher,
Hammersmith*

**The Thames from
Millbank** (2002) by Paul
Simonon (b. 1955), former
bassist of The Clash. This
painting depicts London and
the River Thames and hangs
in the dining room of Locanda
Locatelli. It has a raw energy,
which I find is very beautiful.
Giorgio Locatelli, chef, London

Theatre. Lights go down.
Excitement beats in my chest.
A concentrated frown. The

first actor put to the test.
A lifetime of emotion in an
hour! *Claire Evans, desk
assistant, St Albans*

'Thing'. It may be hard
to tell why this found object
would be wondrous to us.
In fact, it is hard to tell what
this object is. And that, for
us, is the point of this choice.
An unidentifiable bit of
plastic, found at Deptford
junk market, is our offering
as a humble wonder. We
acquired this piece some time
ago and it has since defied
categorisation and
identification. It has an on/off
switch but apparently no
moving parts. It seems to be
fashioned to emulate either
a cloud or a wave of sea water
but one can't be sure which.
It may well be part of a toy,
but it has a flat surface that
might be for a cup or vessel
and it gives no clue as what
might be meant to interact
with it. It has no branding,
wording or instructions on
it and no way to take it apart
without spoiling its integrity,
so its mystery continues.
It does have a compartment
for batteries, which we have
tried, but on switching it on,

nothing happened. Simply, it
inspires wonder, and wonder
not only for what its function
is, but wonder that mankind
has designed, manufactured,
sold and discarded this
strange bit of plastic, and one
can't even tell what it is. *Clare
Page and Harry Richardson,
designers, London*

Thought. I can think
thoughts that take any shape
or form, inventive and
fabulous, and as disturbing
and dark as I like - without
anyone else knowing. *Heesun,
trainee accountant, London*

Thumbs (opposable).
The perfection of the thumb
came to me while opening a
jar of jam. So many things
made possible by a simple
shift of angle. *Emily King,
design writer, London*

Thunderstorms.
*Helen Knowles, prison doctor,
Stamford*

Tiller. My all-time
favourite horse. I galloped

FIG. 29. TOY *Todd Longstaffe-Gowan*

The wonder of my world is
My trainers and Money

FIG. 30. TRAINERS AND MONEY *Year 7 pupil, London*

him at Belmont Park in New York in the early 1980s for David Whiteley, and we got along great. He had been erratic to gallop, but we had some kind of bond. In the two years I breezed him, over any distance, I don't know that I was more than 2/5s of a second off the stopwatch, ever. *Richard Violette, Jr, racehorse trainer, New York*

{PLATE 21}

Toby. He is my wonder. *Clare Shilland, photographer, London*

Tornadoes. The power, the beauty. It is my ambition to travel to the US to storm-chase for a few months. *Pete Crundwell, head chef, Norfolk*

{FIG. 29}

Toy. The conjunction of string, wire, a black monkey skull and the soles from a clapped-out pair of espadrilles does not sound promising. Nonetheless, the result is wholly original and wondrous. This children's toy - more startlingly original than a Picasso - hails from a remote village in Mali. *Todd Longstaffe-Gowan, landscape designer, London*

{FIG. 30}

Trainers and money. *Year 7 pupil, Woolwich Polytechnic School for Boys, London*

Treacy, Philip (b. 1967, milliner). His remarkable galleon hat. *Alannah Weston, creative director, London*

{FIG. 31}

Trees. Trees are plentiful and ancient. Amongst them, you can imagine the world before the marks of humanity had scarred the earth. Here I feel free and truly wonderful. *Toby Shuall, artist and designer, London*

{PLATE 63}

Trial by jury. *Andrew Williams, journalist, London*

Truth and Reconciliation Council, South Africa. Set up by Desmond Tutu to encourage the people of South Africa to forgive each other for the various horrors of apartheid, to trade honesty and truth for revenge. This, beyond all else, I regard as a great wonder of the recent world. It would have been impossible for me to have imagined that it could work - until it did. I see the TRC as one of the greatest imaginative acts of all time, an act of outrageous idealism that paid off. *Brian Eno, artist and musician, London*

Tuc-tuc/Bajaj/Trishaw. Wonders of the Eastern world. Aesthetically

FIG. 31. PHILIP TREACY'S GALLEON HAT *Alannah Weston*

challenged and yet impossibly endearing, combining features from a moped, ski lift and twin-seater propeller plane, their owners still feel obliged to customise their vehicle beyond belief. Surely Western cities could be transformed for the better with such cheap and dinky short-distance public transporters? *Charlie de Bono, architect, London*

Twelve things. Fresh carrots. The one-minute sculptures I make with my daughter, Joy. Erwin Olaf's photograph of a model as Jackie Kennedy. The never-built black copy of the Taj Mahal. Bonsai. Graphic designer Anton Beeke's poster for the KunstRai art fair, with the face of the late designer Benno Premsela. Jaguar F-Type. Sea dragons. Mosaic tiles. Female lips curling up (also called a smile). Vermeer's *Girl with a Pearl Earring*. Philippe Starck's teddy bear. *Marcel Wanders, designer, Amsterdam*

Universe. That the whole universe was once smaller than a walnut, and that we can't really 'see' the majority of it even now. Allows for all sorts of things to be true that we can't fathom yet (and will ensure that in a few hundred years our intelligence and understanding will seem as primitive as the witch-burners'). *Jon Gisby, new media executive, Harpenden*

Ulysees. James Joyce's unattainable novel for all time. *David Allan, reader, London*

Unconditional love. *Amanda Phillips, art dealer, Sydney*

UNIVERSE *Jon Gisby*

Veins on leaves. *Emma, primary school pupil, London*

Venice. City of wonder. Amazing architecture, history and romantic ambience. See Venice before it disappears into the lagoon forever. *Jane, switchboard operator, Leicester*

Verrucas. Who's idea was that? What purpose do they serve? *Laura Hadland, curator, Leicester*

PLATE 46} **Victoria Falls, Zambia.** *Patrice Taylor, retailer, Miami*

VOYNICH MANUSCRIPT

Villa d'Este, Lake Como, Italy. Shelley talked of this lake's beauty and it has changed little since his time. Others have described it as heaven. The gardens and the position of the hotel conjure up images to me of the kind of landcape I dream of finding if I ever do make it to Heaven. *Paula Pryke, florist, London*

Violets. Every year, violets appear in my garden. They seed themselves, and it is always uncertain if any will grow. The tiny plants pop up in Spring in unexpected places – between paving stones, under the hedge. Truly wonderful. *Hilary Bloom, charity director, London*

Vitamin C tablets, plus a pestle and mortar, syringe and beaker. Without them, my best friend, Frodo – a rescued, abused guinea pig – would have died a painful, slow death. *Beverley Andrews, housewife and guinea pig slave, Ilkeston*

Voynich manuscript. An unreadable book with enigmatic illustrations kept in the Beinecke Rare Manuscripts Department of Yale University. There is

no consensus about how old it is. Many people (mostly crackpots) have claimed to have deciphered it, yet it has defeated the world's best cryptographers and linguistic experts. Named after an antiquarian scholar, Wilfrid Voynich, who found it in a Jesuit seminary in Italy, it might be about alchemy, or sexual techniques, or life on other planets, or Christian heresy. It contains drawings of plants, moons and stars and fat, naked women. The whole thing may be a hoax, but computer analysis of the structures and repetitions indicates that this cannot be the case. *Robert Irwin, writer and editor, London*

VEINS ON LEAVES *Emma*

Incipit plogus fratis ieronimi presbiteri: in libros machabeorum.

achabeorum libri duo pnotant prelia: inter hebreos duces gentemq; persarum: pugna qm sabbatos: z nobiles machabei ducis triumphos: ex cui9 noie z libri ijdem sut nucupati. Prec qm historia connet etia iuclita illa gesta machabeor frattu: qui sub antiocho rege pro sacris legibz dira tormenta perpessi sunt. Quos mater pia dum diuersis suppliciis urgeret non solu no fleuit: sed et gaudes hortabat ad gloria passionis. Explicit plog' incipit lib' pm' machabeoru.

Et factu est postqm; percussit alexander philippi rex macedo qui primus regnauit i grecia egressus de terra cethim dariu rege persaru z medos. Obtinuit prelia multa: et obtinuit omniu munitiones: et interfecit reges terre. Et ptasijt usq; ad fines terre: z accepit spolia multitudinis gentiu: z siluit terra i conspectu eius. Et congregauit uirtute z exercitu fortem nimis: et exaltatu est et eleuatu cor ei9: et obtinuit regiones gentiu z tyrannos et facti sunt illi i tributu. Et post hec decidit in lectu: z cognouit quia moreretur. Et uocauit pueros suos nobiles qui secu erant nutriti a iuuentute sua: et diuisit illis regnu suu cum adhuc uiueret. Et regnauit alexander annis duodecim: z mortu9 e. Et obtinuerut pueri ei9 regnu unusquisq; i loco suo: et imposuerut omnes sibi diademata post morte ei9 z filii eor post eos annis multis: et multiplicata sut mala i terra. Et exijt ex eis radix peccati: antiochus

illustris fili9 antiochi regis qui fuerat rome obses: et regnauit in anno centesimotricesimo et septimo regni grecorum. In diebz illis exierunt ex isr' filii iniqui: z suaserut multis dicentes. Eamus z disponamus9 testamentu cu gentibus que circa nos sut: quia exquo recessim9 ab eis inuenerut nos multa mala. Et bonus uisus e sermo i oclis eorx. Et destinauerut aliqui de ppslo z abierut ad rege: et dedit illis potestate ut facere iusticia gentiu. Et edificauerut gymnasiu in therosolimis secdm leges nationu z fecerut sibi ppucia: z recesserut a testameto sancto z iuncti sut nationibz: et uenudati sunt ut facere malu. Et paratu e regnu in conspectu antiochi: z cepit regnare i terra egipti: ut regnaret sup duo regna. Et intrauit in egiptu i multitudine graui in curribus z elephantis z equitibz: z copiosa nauiu multitudine. Et constituit bellu aduersus ptolomeu rege egipti: z ueritus e ptolomeus a facie eius z fugit: et ceciderut uulnerati multi. Et comprehendit ciuitates munitas in terra egipti: z accepit spolia terre egipti. Et conuertit antiochus postqm; puscit egiptu in centesimo z quadragesimo z tercio anno: z ascendit ad isr' et ascendit iherosolimis i multitudine graui. Et intrauit in sanctificatione cu supbia: z accepit altare aureu z candelabru luminis z uniuersa uasa eius z mensam propositionis z libatoria z fialas z mortariola aurea z uelu z coronas z ornamentu aureum qd in facie templi erat: z comminuit oia. Et accepit argentum z auru et uasa concupiscibilia: et accepit thesauros occultos quos inuenit: et sublatis omnibz abijt i terra sua. Et fecit cedem hominu: et locutus est in

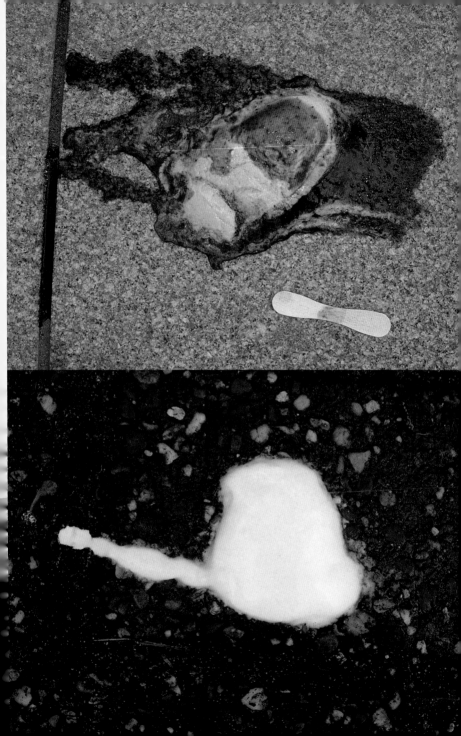

Waste management.
Adam Cowper Smith, cleaning manager, London

Wakeboarding. Bruises and laughter. The freedom on the water is exhilarating. *Irene Allan, marketing manager, Glasgow*

Walkabout (1971).* Compared to most narrative features of its time, this film by Nicolas Roeg is almost wordless. It is the last he is credited with photographing himself. *Robert Hollins, editor, London*

Wallace Collection, London. So many objects of beauty. *Lindsay Treger, negotiator, London*

*Written by Edward Bond, and based on the novel by James Vance Marshall. *Walkabout* starred Jenny Agutter, Luc Roeg (the director's young son) and David Gulpilil. Nominated for the Palme d'Or at the 1971 Cannes festival, *Walkabout* is also cited by Kevin Macdonald as an inspiration for the cinematography in his documentary film *Touching the Void.*

Water. (1) I used to live in northern Kenya, where water was not freely available nor clean. Clean water from a tap is the biggest wonder that most people don't fully appreciate. *Karen Breakell, head of human resources, Crawley* **(2)** An ethereal silvery-white liquid whose every-day appearance belies the fact that this element is responsible for the survival of every single person on the planet. *Natalie Barbosa, legal assistant, Manchester* **(3)** Flows smoothly, yet can be as forceful as steel. Soft, yet used to cut diamonds, the hardest material in the world. Amazing. *Naomi Wood, personal assistant, London*

(4) Colourless, odourless, tasteless – still, you'll never experience it the same way twice. *Julia Castillo, designer, London* **(5)** Because it's the best drink. *Michael Violette, primary school pupil, London* **(6)** Quenches my thirst, keeps me healthy and helps me to relax at the end of the day. *Sarah Williams, customer services agent, Wilmslow* **(7)** Water is always changing.

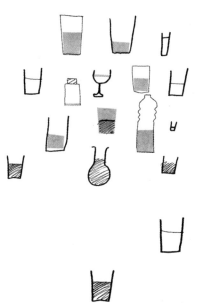

It is totally fluid. I dream that some day my architecture will be as ephemeral as water. *Edwin Chan, architect-designer, Venice, California*

Wikipedia. That self-governing, self-replicating online encyclopaedia fills me with a feverish sense of wonder. Through it we experience something close to our species-mind; pulsing, growing, its tendrils curling up into everything we know or dream of knowing. *David Bain, writer, London*

Wills, Bob (1905–1975), and his Texas Playboys.* One of the great unsung heroes of western popular music, Bob Wills has influenced generations of musicians, Elvis Presley included. *Dave Webster, animator/comic book artist/musician, London*

Man has to awaken to wonder.
–
Ludwig Wittgenstein
(1889–1951)

*In 2007, Bob Wills posthumously received a Grammy Lifetime Achievement Award.

Wine. Glug, glug, glug.
*Oliver Reynolds, amateur
viticulturalist, London*

Wishes. How you want
something so bad and don't
get it, only to find out later
that it would have been a
disaster. Be careful what

*A century ago, historians estimated
that between the 15th and 19th
centuries more than 9 million 'witches'
were put to death. Current estimates
report 100,000 needless executions,
condoned by law or otherwise.

you wish for. *Lylia Crossan,
government officer, Dublin*

Witches.* The ones
among us, I mean, among
our wives and girlfriends and
mothers and sisters. There
are a few, though I don't for a
minute pretend to understand
them. *Michael Curran,
accountant, Hertfordshire*

Wonder, Stevie (b. 1950).†
*Andi Veevers, learning and
development adviser, Trafford*

Wondermentalism. {PLATE 4}
Unexpected, gut-wrenching
hilarity. The miracle of wine.
A look that speaks. Drawings.
The Fall. Generosity. Curves.
Laverda Jota. Speed of light.
'Tomorrow and tomorrow
and tomorrow … etc.'
Friendship. Bigna's arse.
The Garden of Earthly {PLATE 23}
Delights, by H. Bosch.
The lack of any gods. The sun
on fire. The brain. The size
of the universe. The MV
Augusta 750. *Paul Davis,
artist, London*

†Stevie Wonder - born Stevland
Hardaway Judkins - is a singer,
songwriter, musician, recording artist
and producer from Saginaw Michigan.
He first found fame at the age of 11
performing for Berry Gordy's Motown
Records and has since earned 22
Grammy Awards.

During the 1940s and 1950s, publishers Ward, Lock & Co. produced a series of 24 profusely illustrated 'Wonder' books. I possess seven of them: *The Wonder Book of Why and What: Answers to Children's Questions*, *The Wonder Book of Daring Deeds: True Stories of Heroism and Adventure*, *The Wonder Book of the Army*, *The Wonder Book of Science*, *The Wonder Book of Things to Do*, *The Wonder Book of Tell Me Why*, and, finally, *The Wonder Book of Wonders*.

Yet my favourite 'Wonder' book is not part of this series. *The Wonder Gift Book for Children* (Odhams Press, c.1945) was inscribed 'From Uncle Sam,* February 17, 1946' and in it I discovered stories and poems by Stevenson, Belloc, Kipling, de la Mare, Wells and others. I still browse through this book, recapturing something of my childhood enjoyment.

This book also fondly reminds me of my uncle. In 1948, thanks to a £78 win on Littlewoods Football Pools, my family was able to accept uncle Sam's invitation to join him, for a week at Butlin's Holiday Camp in Clacton. This was at the height of the post-war holiday camp boom and it remains, no question, the best holiday of my life. Among other treats, I won first prize in the Children's Talent Contest, singing two popular songs of the day, 'April Showers' and 'I Wonder [there it is again] Who's Kissing Her Now'.

Sitting and knitting and watching benignly was the camp's resident Redcoat songstress. Though off-duty, she was urged on stage by the compère to join me in a reprise of 'I Wonder Who's Kissing Her Now' and when it was over she did something that took me by surprise, something I'd never experienced before. She kissed me full on the mouth. It was strangely and profoundly thrilling, and, in combination with the audience's applause, altogether wonderful. Could this have had anything to do, I wonder, with the fact that I eventually took to the stage professionally? Or that I spent much of my adolescence trying to find out more about this kissing lark? As for Clacton's Redcoat songstress, I wonder who's kissing her now.

I suppose these experiences aren't strictly contemporary, but they're still part of me and I'm still here in 2007 - a source of wonderment in itself.

Neil Hornick, editor/archivist/performance artist, London

*My uncle Sam was actually my great-uncle, and father of Harry Gold, bass sax virtuoso and leader of the Pieces of Eight, a popular band that I often heard on the radio during the late 1940s. In 1995, they played in person at my 25th wedding anniversary.

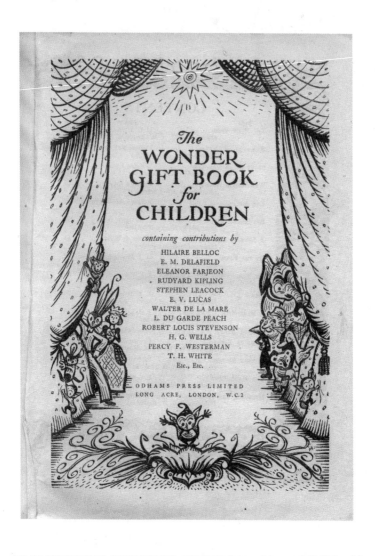

The
WONDER
GIFT BOOK
for
CHILDREN

containing contributions by

HILAIRE BELLOC
E. M. DELAFIELD
ELEANOR FARJEON
RUDYARD KIPLING
STEPHEN LEACOCK
E. V. LUCAS
WALTER DE LA MARE
L. DU GARDE PEACH
ROBERT LOUIS STEVENSON
H. G. WELLS
PERCY F. WESTERMAN
T. H. WHITE
Etc., Etc.

ODHAMS PRESS LIMITED
LONG ACRE, LONDON, W.C.2

FIG. 32. THE WONDER GIFT BOOK FOR CHILDREN (DETAIL) (C. 1945) *Neil Hornick*

WUNDERKAMMERN

For a good century
and a half after the discovery
of America, Europe's *mind was blown.*
That was the animating spirit behind, and
the enduring significance of, the profusion of
Wunderkammern. It wasn't just the American (or,
alternatively, African, Far Eastern, Greenlandian,
etc.) artifacts that they displayed (phosphorescent
feathers, shrunken heads, rhinoceros horns). It
was how the palpable reality of such artifacts
so vastly expanded the territory
of the now readily
conceivable. Horns, for example,
were suddenly all the rage – rhinoceros horns,
unicorn horns, sea unicorn horns … human horns, dainty
round horns coming sprouting out of proper Englishwomen's
foreheads, for God's sake! But rhinoceros horns *were* real; and
sea unicorns *did* exist (in the form, anyway, of narwhals, with
those uncannily spiralling unitary tusks seemingly protruding
from out of their foreheads) – so why couldn't unicorn horns
or even human horns exist as well? Our great-grandfathers'
certainties, debunked by our grandfathers, were
suddenly turning out to be not quite so
easily debunkable after all.

To give another example,
consider the testimony of Edward Brown, from his
1673 monograph *A Brief Account of some Travels in divers
Parts of Europe …* (I'll spare you the full title, which goes on for
another whole paragraph), who records that while in Leipzig
he visited the Burgomeister, one Herr von Adlershelme,
'a courteous Lerned Person, and great virtuoso, who
has collected and observed many things,'

and who had gathered together in his
'Chamber of Rarities' many things that were -
the word Brown uses is 'considerable'. Promising to
confine his own list to 'but a few', Brown then
goes on to enumerate:

'An Elephant's Head
with the dentes molares *in it. An*
Animal like an Armadillo, but the scales
are much larger and the Tail broader. Very large
flying Fishes. A Seahorse. Bread of Mount Libanus.
A Cedar branch with the Fruit upon it. Large Granates
as they grow in the Mine. A Siren's hand. A Chameleon.
A piece of Iron, which seems to be the head of a Spear,
found in the Tooth of an Elephant, the Tooth being grown
about it. The Isle of Jersey drawn by our King Charles the
Second. A piece of wood with the Blood of King Charles
the First upon it. A Greenland Lance with a large Bell
at the end of it. Much Japan painting, wherein their
manner of hunting and working may be observed.
A Picture of our Saviour [upon] the Hatches [of]
which are ... written ... the Story of his Passion.
Bevers taken in the River Elbe. A Picture
of the murther of the Innocents,
done by Albrecht Dürer. ...'

A bloody piece of wood, a stuffed beaver,
an elephant's tusk, a siren's hand, a bridal garter
and a painting by Dürer - not an untypical trove. Nor is it
untypical for the provenance of many of what we today
consider Renaissance and Baroque masterpieces to
wend their way back through the hodgepodge
of collections such as these.

Lawrence Weschler, author of *Mr Wilson's
Cabinet of Wonders: Pronged Ants, Horned Humans and
Other Marvels of Jurassic Technology*, New York

WORMS *Sophie Groves*

Woodpeckers. Rarely seen, but beautiful. I'm no twitcher, but it's wonderful to open the curtains and see one feeding in the garden. *Ann-Marie, brand manager, Windsor*

World peace. Humankind's innate ability to survive against all odds: where hope never dies and there's peace on Earth, the wonder of no war. *Dawn Henderson, education adviser, Chorlton*

Worms. Some worms eat themselves if they can't find any food. *Sophie Groves, recruitment agent, Leicester*

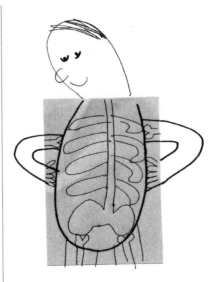

{PLATE 58} **Xi'an's Terracotta Army, Shaanxi Province, China.** Buried with the first Emperor of Qin, who united China more than 2,000 years ago, this army of more than 8,000 like-like, life-sized warriors is a surviving wonder of the ancient world – and one of the earliest examples of Chinese mass production. The scale is awe-inspiring, an imaginative feat made almost-real. *Simon Willis, creative director, London*

X-ray. How do you point something that you can't see at a person and then see their bones on a picture you have to hold to the light? It's illogical. If it was invented on a TV show you'd laugh at it, it just sounds ludicrous. *Anna Skelton,* student services administrator, Liverpool*

*Anna Skelton's other wonders include Archimedes' shield (p. 6) and: 'The sounds of ducks quacking - it's just such a happy, happy sound you can't be sad when you hear it. Kissing - why have all societies discovered kissing? When you think about it, it's weird and generally icky. Sundials - how did somebody think "I'll put a small pole up and some marks around it and tell time!" Come to think of it, who invented the measurements of time? Who decided what an hour was and why do minutes and seconds come in 60s rather than nice round hundreds? Why do people have accents? Why do you 'pick up' an accent if you're in that place for a while? Why don't you pick up an accent from watching TV?'

165

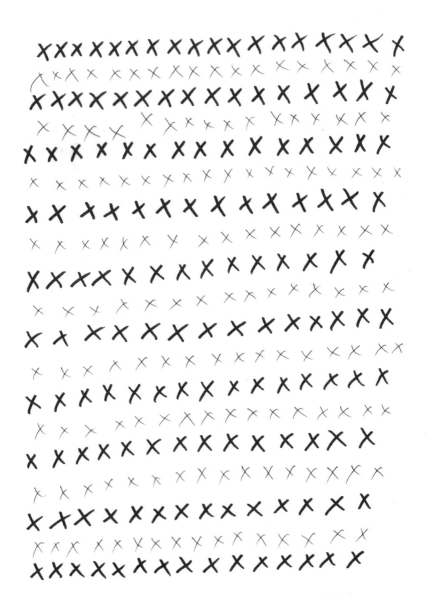

X (KISSES)

Yeast. I make bread about twice a week, yet I never get over the wonder of seeing dough rise. And I often think of all the hard work the yeast does before I destroy it in a hot oven! Many years ago, watcing ginger beer fermenting nicely in my under-sink cupboard gave me the same pleasure. *Marie-Joṡèphe Pradere, research nurṡe, Mancheṡter*

Yes Men. The Yes Men are led by two Americans who cunningly deceive the corporate world (and even BBC World) in their endeavour to show the unfair differences between first-, second- and third-world economies. The wonder is that they actually succeeded to expose indifference to unfairness. They started by making a

website very similar to the World Trade Organisation's site (WTO) and one similar to President Bush's website. Because of that, they got invited to express their thoughts at conferences on the web and on TV. Instead of declining, they accepted the invitations and tried to expose some of the WTO's unfair policies - not by describing injustices, but by exaggerating the ideas of the WTO to enrage the participants and wake them up. Surprisingly, their audiences dozed and yawned as usual. Still, the Yes Men expose how extremely unfair policies can exist without being criticised - evidently no one cares or even listens at all. *Emeline Coṡijnṡe, deṡigner, Eindhoven*

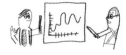

Yorkshire. My escape, my profound admiration, the wonder of my world: the ever-changing view from my home in the Yorkshire countryside. *Christopher Bailey, designer, London*

Youth cultures. Spotty, recalcitrant, terrifying in packs and yet the cornerstone of much

that makes London such an exciting city. Inventive, immediate, idealistic, frequently immature, and communicative in a way that is impenetrable to everyone else, 'youth cultures' can sweep you away on a tide of exhilaration and bright-eyed envy. *Simon Willis, creative director, London*

Zeitgeist. A simple, fleeting moment that is personal and special only to those who were there, and completely trivial to anyone who wasn't. A memory. A zeitgeist that brings a smile to your face and fills you with joy. A scene where the bad and normal parts of the day are strained away leaving only the good in an exaggerated, almost unreal form. Detail is reduced. People's reactions are heightened. Context becomes hazy there to clarify the theatre but the specifics of which are long forgotten. *Scott Bradley, advertising executive, London*

Zyxin. Look it up. A real word beginning with the last three letters of the alphabet. How wonderful is that? *Simon Willis, creative director, London*

169

INDEX OF CONTRIBUTORS

*Where the surname or occupation of a contributor is unknown
or was not supplied to the editors, none is given. Page references are
indicated in roman, figures in italic and colour plates in bold.
Identical surnames do not necessarily indicate family relations.*

Y

AFTERWORD

*Wonder, /'wʌndə/ n. a feeling of surprise and admiration,
caused by something beautiful, unexpected, or unfamiliar.*
Oxford English Dictionary

Develop imagination; throw away routine.
Gordon Selfridge (1858-1947)

Two years ago, a few of us began to explore the idea of creating
a room of 'wonder' at Selfridges. Inspired by the notion of a
wunderkammer, or cabinet of curiosities, it would be a place
full of rare and precious things. It would be home to the finest
jewellers, watchmakers and winemakers in the world, but it
would also be a place to discover wonders of another kind: a
book on clouds, a transparent chessboard, a diamond studded
toilet plunger, a miniature coffin - all things you had no idea
you were searching for until you found them.

So - to mark the opening of the Wonder Room - we have
commissioned *A Book of Wonder*. A kind of *wunderkammer* of
its own, between its covers lie the esoteric and the every-day, the
natural and the technological, the sublime and the ridiculous.
Like the *wunderkammern* of the past, this collection doesn't
have a particular theory to support, except perhaps to show that
not only is the world is full of wonders but (and perhaps more
importantly) our sense of wonder is alive and well.

Alannah Weston, Creative Director, Selfridges, August 2007

PHOTOGRAPHIC CREDITS (PLATES)

1. Pictorial Press Ltd/Alamy
2. David Noton Photography/Alamy
3. The Flight Collection/Alamy
4. Paul Davis (contributor's own)
5. Ronan and Erwan Bouroullec (contributor's own)
6. Emilia Bairamova (contributor's own)
7. EMPICS Sports Photo Agency
8. Adrian Muttitt/Alamy
9. CERN, Geneva
10. The Israel Museum, Jerusalem, Israel/Vera & Arturo Schwarz Collection of Dada and Surrealist Art/ The Bridgeman Art Library/© Succession Marcel Duchamp/ADAGP, Paris and DACS, London 2007
11. Bruce Coleman Inc./Alamy
12. Graham Mancha (contributor's own)
13. Unknown, courtesy John Baxter (contributor)
14. Jean-Philippe Arles/Reuters/Corbis
15. Getty Images
16. Susan Deere (contributor's own)
17. Gary Cook/Alamy
18. Bettina Von Hase (contributor's own)
19. CAIDA/Science Photo Library
20. Blickwinkel/Alamy
21. Claire Shilland (contributor's own)
22. Juniors Bildarchiv/Alamy
23. Akg-images
24. Steven Georges/Press-Telegram/ Corbis
25. Smithsonian Institution/Corbis
26. PEANUTS © United Feature Syndicate, Inc.
27. Bettmann/Corbis
28. PCL/Alamy
29. JTB Photo Communications, Inc./Alamy
30. Jeremy Tracy (contributor's own)
31. Nick Thornton-Jones and Warren Du Preez (contributors' own)
32. Museum of Jurassic Technology, Los Angeles
33. Chris Petersen (contributor's own)
34. Eddie Gerald/Alamy
35. PA photos
36. Marina McQuade (contributor's own)
37. Woodfall Wild Images/Alamy
38. Garry Penny/epa/Corbis
39. Corinne Quin (contributor's own)
40. (clockwise from top) Philipp Wichtl; Magnus Pettersson; Jo Walton; Marianne Noble; Pictorial Press Ltd/Alamy
41. Peter Turnley/Corbis
42. Anne Deniau (contributor's own)
43. Susan Cook (contributor's own)
44. Alison Smith (contributor's own)
45. Massimo Listri/Corbis
46. Louise Gubb/Corbis Saba
47. Paul Souders|WorldFoto/Alamy
48. Tim Graham/Corbis
49. Yvette Cardozo/Alamy
50. Akg-images/Erich Lessing
51. HBO/The Kobal Collection/ Wetcher, Barry
52. Lucinda Noble (contributor's own)
53. Steve Bloom Images/Alamy
54. Mike Radcliffe (contributor's own)
55. Jim Sugar/Corbis
56. Mike Lane/NHPA
57. Dave Bartruff/Corbis
58. Keren Su/Corbis
59. Jon Arnold Images/Alamy
60. Jim Zuckerman/Alamy
61. Akg-images
62. Akg-images
63. Toby Shuall (contributor's own)
64. Marti Guixé (contributor's own)
65. Robert Violette
66. Andrew Putler/Redferns
67. Alamy
68. Leslie Garland Picture Library/Alamy

PHOTOGRAPHIC CREDITS (FIGURES)

1. Joe Cosco / © The Metropolitan Museum of Art
2. Mary Evans Picture Library/Alamy
3. INTERFOTO Pressebildagentur/Alamy
4. Qingsong Wang (contributor's own)
5. Pictorial Press Ltd/Alamy
6. Sunset Boulevard/Corbis
7. Annette Messager (contributor's own)
8. Chris Moore/Hussein Chalayan
9. Andreas Murray (contributor's own)
10. Courtesy Erdem (photography: Simon Lipman; fashion and direction: Gasha Miladinovic; make-up: Philipp Uberfellner; hair: Michiko Nakamura)
11. Courtesy Lisa Santi
12. The Ronald Grant Archive
13. Kerr|Noble
14. Fortean Picture Library
15. Unknown, courtesy John Baxter (contributor)
16. Medical-on-Line/Alamy
17. Bryan Adams (contributor's own)
18. Beth Derbyshire (contributor's own)
19. Sweet Charity Universal Pictures/Ronald Grant Archive
20. Bruce Weber/Little Bear Inc.
21. Robin Catchpole (contributor's own)
22. Alison Jackson (contributor's own)
23. © Royal Geographical Society
24. James and James
25. Edwin Levick/The Mariners' Museum/Corbis
26. Akg-images
27. Sarah Whittington (contributor's own)
28. Hulton-Deutsch Collection/Corbis
29. Todd Longstaffe-Gowan (contributor's own)
30. Year 7 pupil (contributor's own)
31. Bruce Weber/Little Bear Inc.
32. Neil Hornick (contributor's own)

LIST OF PLATES

(contributor name in italic)

ix